How to Pass

Manuscript Transcription

How to Pass

Manuscript
Transcription

LCCI
LONDON
CHAMBER
of
COMMERCE &
INDUSTRY
COMMERCIAL
EDUCATION
TRUST
EXAMINATIONS
BOARD

Shirley Taylor

M&E

Macdonald & Evans
128 Long Acre, London WC2E 9AN

A Division of Pearson Professional Limited

First published in Great Britain in 1995

ISBN 0 7121 0871 8

British Library Cataloguing in Publication Data
A CIP catalogue record for this book can be obtained from the British Library

10 9 8 7 6 5 4 3 2 1

Typeset by 🖋 Tek Art, Croydon, Surrey
Printed and bound in Great Britain by Bell and Bain Ltd, Glasgow

The Publishers' policy is to use paper manufactured from sustainable forests.

Contents

Preface

As a trainee secretary or one who is retraining to develop and improve their skills, you are on the brink of a very exciting era. Over the past few years the secretary's role has developed tremendously. In today's fast-changing technological times, with computers on the desks of both executives and secretaries, this transformation is set to continue.

To meet the challenges of this exciting time, flexibility, accuracy and time management are essential. You must be assertive and energetic so that you can juggle priorities while dealing with an ever-expanding range of tasks and responsibilities.

As an integral part of the management team, you will be right there on the front line, expected to overcome daily challenges with calm efficiency. You will manage executives' expensive time and influence new business. Furthermore, you must continue to make maximum contribution to your organisation by taking advantage of any available opportunities to develop your skills and discover new potential.

As technology is developing, so too are global business opportunities. As a secretary in an international, multicultural business environment, it is essential that you appreciate the special skills required. In particular, to operate efficiently in this key position, effective communication skills are essential. Even though much of your time will be spent communicating on the telephone or dealing personally with colleagues and business contacts, printed communication will also play a major part in almost every aspect of your job.

Traditionally regarded as a company's ambassador, business letters convey an impression of the company in the way they are displayed, the quality and printing of the letterheaded paper and the language and tone used. High standards in a company's external correspondence have traditionally suggested similarly high standards in business generally.

However, with technological developments now facilitating instant communication all over the world, speed has become the key to successful business negotiations. Unfortunately, this sense of urgency seems to have resulted in a decline in the standard of printed business communications.

At the same time, in a constant battle for 'quality', many companies have invested a great deal of money in campaigns designed to improve their provision of goods and services. Sadly, however, similar 'quality' treatment does not seem to have been given to printed communications.

In today's competitive world, setting high 'quality' standards is of paramount importance, but so too is realising that such 'quality' would be enhanced by good communication standards. It is here you have a vital role to play. In such a key position, it is your duty to try to improve communication between colleagues and business contacts. By setting high standards in the important area of communication – whether verbal, screen-based or printed – you will be helping to create and enhance the corporate image of your organisation. You will also be increasing your value to the company and playing a major part in its success.

As technological developments continue, so too does the potential for business expansion. Your aim must be to grow with these technological changes and to constantly improve your skills. By keeping up-to-date with technological innovations you will expand your responsibilities and hopefully increase your management involvement.

While meeting the exciting challenges of this fast-paced, ever-changing business world, it is important that you accept responsibility for ensuring that these constant technological developments do not result in a decline in communication standards. You have a responsibility to maintain the quality standards of printed communication in your organisation, and to seek ways of developing your skills to ensure that such quality is maintained.

Shirley Taylor

Introduction

The ability to produce typewritten business documents from written instructions is a quality required by more and more employers today. The practical nature of this book aims to help the secretary in developing the essential skills involved in manuscript transcription.

Assignments have been carefully separated and graded with the aim of gradually improving comprehension, enhancing initiative and developing the high standards of composition and presentation which are essential in all typewritten/word processed communications.

Objective

This book is designed to help candidates preparing for the LCCI Examinations Board Second and/or Third Level Manuscript Transcription Examination whether they are Full Award candidates for the Secretarial Studies Certificate/Private Secretary's Certificate or Component Entry candidates.

After working systematically through this book, candidates should be able to approach these examinations with confidence.

Integration

This book sets standards for all typewritten business communications. However, it must be remembered that Manuscript Transcription is just one component of the Group Secretarial Awards. Some of the documents studied in Manuscript Transcription are also included in the syllabuses of other examinations:

- Office Procedures (SSC)
- Office Organisation and Secretarial Procedures (PSC)
- Communication – Use of English (SSC and PSC)

An example of this is the subject of arranging meetings. In Office Organisation and Secretarial Procedures the subject of arranging meetings is studied from the viewpoint of the secretary. In Communication – Use of English, it is necessary to compose meetings documentation. In Manuscript Transcription it is necessary to compose and type these documents. Similarly, several other documents overlap between various examinations – for example memos, advertisements, job descriptions, invitations and itineraries.

The relationship between the components of the examinations has been developed because of the wide-ranging nature of the secretary's role. As such, it is essential to ensure that each component is not treated in isolation during training. The aim must be to ensure co-operation from teacher to teacher and consistency from subject to subject. Teachers of individual components who co-operate with each other by agreeing on standardised methods and a common approach will be helping their students to achieve examination success.

Organisation

This a comprehensive workbook which may be used in class or for self-study.

Part A Written Communication Today looks at the principles of good business communications, including structure and language, together with a checklist for successful communications.

Part B Production Requirements illustrates specimen formats for the most commonly-used documents.

Part C The Workbook helps candidates to appreciate acceptable and appropriate display of material. It also develops the unique skills required in the Manuscript Transcription examination. Each section contains worked assignments, marked answers, analysis of candidates' work, general transcription tips, and pointers to aid transcription of individual assignments.

Part D The Examination brings together all the skills developed so far. The main reasons for penalties are summarised. Guidelines are given to ensure examination success. A complete examination paper is analysed and a candidate's answers are marked. On a second examination paper, pointers are given to help with transcription of each assignment. Further practice is provided by the inclusion of complete examination papers.

Suggested answers to some of the assignments are provided in the book. It should be noted that these are not 'model answers' but 'check copies', examples of work which interprets the employer's intentions accurately and appropriately.

When to use this workbook

Before beginning work on this book students should have developed keyboarding proficiency to at least 25/30 wpm. They should be competent in the presentation of most common business documents and should have good proofreading and error-correction skills.

Timing

The best results will be achieved by working systematically through the book. However, some students will progress faster than others. For guidance, it is felt that approximately 25–30 hours are necessary to work through Part C The Workbook, with another 15–20 hours for Part D The Examination.

It is hoped that the illustrative, step-by-step approach of this workbook will help students to develop the skills required to achieve success in the Manuscript Transcription examination. It is also hoped that the emphasis on clear and consistent presentation will encourage secretaries in training to set high quality standards in all communications.

Part A

Written communication today

This book aims to help you pass the Manuscript Transcription examination. However, in working through the assignments you will also be indirectly helping yourself to pass other examinations. In particular, there is a close relationship between Manuscript Transcription and Communication – Use of English.

In both exams you will be given instructions regarding composition of written business communications. You will be expected to choose the appropriate display and to ensure that all the essential information is included in the message. You must also ensure appropriate use of language, including vocabulary, grammar, spelling and punctuation.

However, while it is hoped that the exercises in this book will complement the work carried out in Communication – Use of English lessons, the emphasis here is, of course, on the requirements of the Manuscript Transcription examination.

Despite the close relationship of Manuscript Transcription with the exam Communication – Use of English, it is not intended that this section examines in depth the principles involved in effective communications. However, it will be useful at the outset to look briefly at some of the basic techniques involved. The importance of structuring documents logically and some general rules of good business writing will also be discussed. Finally there is a checklist for successful communications.

Unit 1

Getting the message across

> By the end of this unit you will be able to:
>
> ● *appreciate the general principles of composing good business communications using appropriate style*
>
> ● *appreciate the importance of ensuring that all business communications follow a logical structure*

The fast-paced nature of today's business world means that higher standards of understandable written business communications have become increasingly important. Good written communication results when you say exactly what you want to say clearly, concisely and in the appropriate tone.

In all communications grammatical structure, good punctuation and spelling are essential. However, more than an ability to structure sentences correctly is needed; effective communication involves transferring thoughts and ideas from one person to another. In any communication you must remember that you are not only dealing with a situation, but with a person. The document chosen to convey the information, and the approach and tone used, will be determined by the person who will read the document.

These three main features of any communication are illustrated in this diagram:

The writer

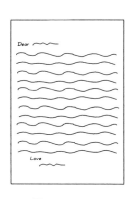

The message

The recipient

Whichever method of communication you choose to convey the message, the following points should be remembered:

1 Choose the means of communication carefully

2 Create the document with care

3 Ensure the document looks good and conveys an image of efficiency and reliability

4 Use a format which is easy to read and structured logically

5 Use a tone appropriate to the circumstances, considering the message, the recipient and the sender

6 Ensure your message is free from grammatical and typographical errors

Techniques of good writing

It has become universally accepted that the language used in business today should be simple, courteous, relaxed and straightforward. The emphasis is firmly on brevity and conciseness while remaining courteous and professional. The ability to write well takes time and experience. However, the positive results achieved with effective communication will make developing the skills worthwhile.

It is the overall style of the communication that will create the initial impression. Unless an appropriate style is used, it will not meet the desired objective.

The two main factors which affect the style of a communication are:

● The relationship between the writer and the reader(s)

● The objective you wish to achieve by sending the communication

When you have given consideration to these two factors, you must then make sure that the style used in composing the message matches the circumstances of the communication. Your aim must be to express yourself so that the message is received and understood with unmistakable clarity in the spirit in which it is intended.

The style used will vary from one communication to another, and will depend on what you wish to achieve. However, a number of general principles will apply, whatever the objective. All communications should be:

Complete   The message should include as much detail as necessary, with no glaring omissions but also no superfluous 'padding'.

Brief	Long-winded messages are less readable and less effective, so plan carefully before committing anything to paper. Use appropriate language, keep sentences short and use simple expressions rather than elaborate phrases.
Clear	Use plain English, with simple and appropriate language. With an easy, natural style, your written communications should not be too formal or too familiar.
Accurate	Include all relevant details, check facts carefully and proofread thoroughly.
Logically structured	Paragraphs should be structured logically. Each one should develop from the last, progressing to a conclusion.
Reader-friendly	Put yourself in the reader's place. The language and structure should help their understanding of the message and should ensure an appropriate response.

Your aim should be to present all the facts and information in a style which encourages the desired response. Ensuring all communications meet these objectives may seem a big responsibility, but the art of effective communication is a skill which can be developed.

Structuring your communications

Most business documents should follow a similar format, with the content flowing logically from beginning to end.

In the examination, as in the office, your employer may not automatically structure messages logically. You must use your initiative to ensure all details are presented in a logical sequence. You may be required to rearrange the notes and move points around so that they link with other related details. In order to do this, you must first of all read through the instructions carefully and consider the purpose of the communication. When you have checked through all the points to be included in the message, ask yourself if any of the points need moving around in order to improve the structure.

Most documents can be structured using this four-point plan:

I Introduction

The first paragraph will state the reason for the communication. It may:

1   acknowledge previous correspondence.

2   refer to a meeting or contact.

3   give background details regarding the issue concerned.

2 Central section

This section will be the main part of the communication which either gives or requests information, sometimes both. The relevant details should be stated clearly and arranged logically, using separate paragraphs for individual points.

3 Conclusion (or response)

The main body should lead automatically to a conclusion. This may be:

1   action you will take as a result of the circumstances mentioned.

2   a response you wish the reader to make as a result of the details provided.

4 Close

The closing sentence or paragraph should be appropriate to the response required; eg 'I hope to hear from you soon.' 'I look forward to meeting you at the conference.'

Example of a badly-structured letter

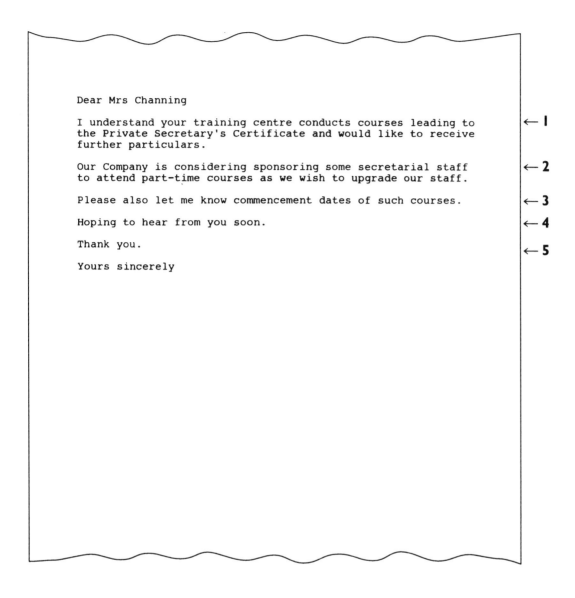

Dear Mrs Channing

I understand your training centre conducts courses leading to
the Private Secretary's Certificate and would like to receive
further particulars.   ← 1

Our Company is considering sponsoring some secretarial staff
to attend part-time courses as we wish to upgrade our staff.   ← 2

Please also let me know commencement dates of such courses.   ← 3

Hoping to hear from you soon.   ← 4

Thank you.   ← 5

Yours sincerely

Key

1 The opening sentence is too long. It includes both the introduction stating the reason for the letter (opening) and also states the action required (response).

2 The second paragraph (again one long sentence) would be better if it was restructured to mention upgrading first and then mention sponsorship.

3 The third paragraph states more details required from the reader. The action mentioned in paragraph one should be linked to this section.

4 Avoid errors like this by starting with 'I' or 'We'. This is not a complete sentence.

5 Phrases like 'Thank you' or 'Kind regards' are unnecessary. A more appropriate closing sentence should be composed. But note, 'With best wishes' is acceptable if the employer wishes to close with a personal touch.

This letter should have been rearranged so that the content falls into the four-point format previously discussed, with each point developing from the last.

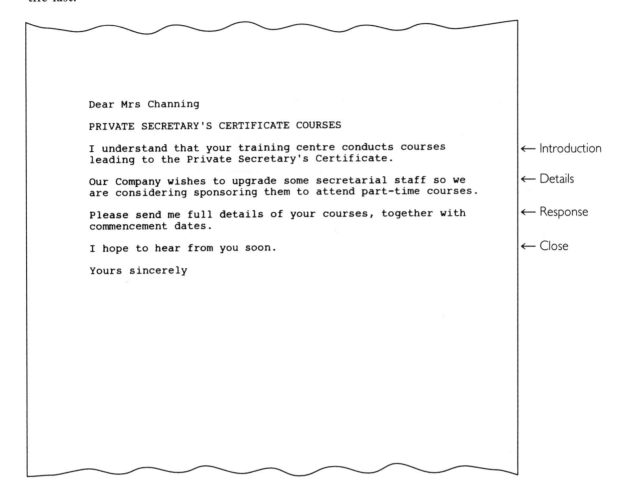

Dear Mrs Channing

PRIVATE SECRETARY'S CERTIFICATE COURSES

I understand that your training centre conducts courses leading to the Private Secretary's Certificate.   ← Introduction

Our Company wishes to upgrade some secretarial staff so we are considering sponsoring them to attend part-time courses.   ← Details

Please send me full details of your courses, together with commencement dates.   ← Response

I hope to hear from you soon.   ← Close

Yours sincerely

Now it's your turn . . .

The following sentences, when rearranged, make a perfectly-structured memo. Put the sentences into their correct order, and do not forget to create paragraphs. Send the memo to Pamela Tyler (Secretarial Services Supervisor) from Eileen Forrest (General Manager). Use the heading NEW TELEPHONE EXCHANGE. NB: You may want to check the suggested memo format first on page 19.

● Full training, will, of course, be provided.

● Please let me have their names before 5 March.

● It is proposed to employ 2 operators on a rota system covering the hours from 0800 to 1800.

● If you have any queries please let me know.

● It has been decided to install a new telephone exchange so that communication links with branches are improved.

● Could you please recommend 3 or 4 candidates from your department who would be willing to train as operators of the new exchange.

Compare your answers with the check copy shown on page 170.

Business language

The secret of composing good business communications is to use plain language, as if you were having a 'conversation in writing'. However, this does not mean you should use long-winded phrases or jargon. Your aim should be to put the message across in a natural way, using a courteous, informal style.

Some basic rules of effective business communications are:

Come straight to the point

Instead of	*Say*
Please be informed that the car park will be closed between 0900 and 1200.	The car park will be closed between 0900 and 1200.
I wish to let you know that an induction course will be held on Monday 1 June.	An induction course will be held on Monday 1 June.
This is to inform you that I will be leaving for my trip to Europe next Tuesday.	I leave for my trip to Europe next Tuesday 7 November.
I would also like to tell you that I will be visiting several of our major clients.	I will also be visiting several major clients.
Would you be so kind as to let me know . . .	Please let me know . . .
I would like to remind you that . . .	Please note that . . . or please remember that . . .
I am so sorry to have to point out that unfortunately we do not have these goods in stock at the present moment in time.	Unfortunately we are out of stock of this item.

Use modern expressions

Instead of	*Say*
I acknowledge receipt of your letter of 2 May.	Thank you for your letter of 2 May.
Enclosed herewith you will see I am sending . . .	I enclose . . .

Instead of	*Say*
I am writing with reference to your letter dated 1 May reference FT/PG451 in which you requested information about training courses provided by our Company.	Thank you for your letter of 1 May enquiring about our training courses.
I have great pleasure in being able to enclose herewith . . .	I enclose . . .
This is to confirm as I told you on the telephone that I wish to reserve the conference room . . .	I confirm reservation of the conference room . . .

Be specific

Instead of	*Say*
I am enclosing the usual information leaflets . . .	I am enclosing some information leaflets on Comlon Chocolate.
The courses were very popular last year.	The assertiveness training courses were very popular last year.
I am pleased to report that all the arrangements for my trip have now been finalised and I will be leaving next week.	The arrangements for my trip to Cyprus are now finalised and I leave next Friday 8 March.
Enclosed is a copy of my draft itinerary.	I enclose a copy of the draft itinerary for my trip to Cyprus and Malta.

Include all essential information

Instead of	*Say*
Our Personnel Officer will contact you soon.	Mr James Wilson, our Personnel Officer, will contact you soon.
My flight arrives around 0800.	My flight SQ101 arrives at London Heathrow Airport at 0815 on Tuesday 7 May.
I really liked the article which you sent to me recently.	I really liked the article on time management which you sent to me recently.

Be consistent

Instead of	*Say*
I confirm the reservation of a single room on 16 February and a double room on 17.2.95.	I confirm the reservation of a single room on 16 February and a double room on 17 February.
The committee will comprise Jean Listiyani, S Kaur and Mrs Simmons.	The committee will comprise Jean Listiyani, Shariffah Kaur and Della Simmons.
In 3 weeks I will be leaving for a two week cruise to Barbados.	In 3 weeks I will be leaving for a 2–week cruise to Barbados.
The color of the furnishings needs changing. A darker colour is needed.	The colour of the furnishings needs to be changed. A darker colour is needed.

Use appropriate tone

Instead of	*Say*
Your washer's guarantee has run out so you must pay for all repairs.	Unfortunately the guarantee on your washer has expired so you will be responsible for any repair costs.
I am writing to complain because I am very angry with the way your staff treated me in your store yesterday.	I was most unhappy with the quality of service I received yesterday.
If you read our brochure properly and follow the instructions on page 21 your problem would be solved.	You will resolve this problem by connecting the fax machine to the answerphone as illustrated on page 21.
Our conference suite is fully booked during September so we cannot fit you in.	Unfortunately there are no available dates during September, but several Saturdays in October are available.

A checklist for successful communications

As a trainee secretary you can develop your own communications skills by reading and studying as many examples of good business communications as possible. You should also study all the letters and other documents you receive, both personally and in the office. Be constructive in your criticism and ask yourself how they compare with the guidelines in this unit and throughout this book.

Ask yourself the following questions:

1   Will it be understood?

2   Does it sound natural and sincere?

3   Is the tone right?

4   Are all the details accurate?

5   Is all the essential information included?

6   Is it clear, concise and courteous?

7   Are all the spellings correct?

8   Is it properly punctuated and grammatically correct?

9   Is it structured logically?

10   Does it look attractive, well-displayed and consistent?

For any written business communication to be successful, you should answer the questions above with a 'yes'.

(Checklist reproduced from *Model Business Letters*, Gartside revised by Taylor, Pitman Publishing)

Part B

Production requirements

The correspondence and documents you will be required to produce in the examination, as in the office, will depend on the nature of the company's business as well as the job title and responsibilities of your employer.

Many companies like to ensure standardisation by adopting their own 'house style' for document layouts. You will not be penalised in an examination for using your house style as long as you use the same format throughout the examination.

The easiest and most popular layout is fully-blocked with open punctuation. This has been used in all the examples shown throughout this book.

Unit 2

Specimen document formats

By the end of this unit you will be able to:

● *appreciate the importance of correct and consistent display of all business documents*

Many of the documents which may be required in the examination are illustrated here. Remember that this list is not exhaustive and you may be required to produce any document which would be expected of a secretary in the business world.

Alongside each document notes have been made covering anything the examiners might be looking out for.

Although it is the presentation that is highlighted in this Unit, remember also that these are also examples of well-written communications. Study the paragraphing, the structure, the language and tone used. This will help you when composing your own documents.

It is assumed that you will study the theoretical aspects of all business documents in Communication – Use of English. You are advised to refer to the textbook *Communication for Business – A Practical Approach, second edition*, which takes a more detailed look at all forms of written business communication. It also contains many practical assignments aimed at developing composition skills.

Business letter

Comlon International plc letterheaded paper should be used for business letters. Margins should be aligned with the start of the printed letterheading. If using a word processor, you may make a template of the Comlon letterhead.

Comlon International plc

Comlon House West Street London SW1Y 2AR

tel: 0181 302 0261
telex: Comlond 888941   telemessages: Comlond London SW1   fax: 0181 302 4169

DA/ST   ← dictator / typist reference

15 June 19--   ← date

Mr Craig Tomkinson   ← inside address, including
Manager   courtesy title and full
Goodison Hotel   details either from
42 St Michael's Drive   incoming document or
Leeds   Instruction Sheet
LS1 9EG

Dear Mr Tomkinson   ← follow instructions given
                                                                                                or compose suitable
I was very pleased to meet you at last week's Business Exhibition in Birmingham.   salutation
As promised, I have pleasure in enclosing our latest brochure on Comlon Seminars
and Conferences.

You will remember we discussed the one-week conference which Comlon is arranging
for a multi-national organisation. This will be held from 11 to 15 December, 1000 to
1700 Monday to Thursday and 1000 to 1230 on the Friday. It is anticipated that
200 delegates will attend.

A copy of our conference specification is attached giving full particulars including our
requirements for refreshments and meals.

I would appreciate receiving full details of your conference accommodation as soon as
possible, together with an estimate of the costs involved and specimen menus.

I hope to hear from you soon.

Yours sincerely   ← appropriate
                                                                                                complimentary close
                                                                                                (to match salutation)

DOUGLAS ALLEN   ← name / designation as
Director   shown on Instruction
Comlon Seminars and Conferences   Sheet

Enc   ← indicate enclosures by
                                                                                                showing Enc or Encs
Copy to Mr Todd Sutcliffe, Conference Manager   ← indicate routing of
                                                                                                copies

---

Personal letter

If the employer wants you to produce a personal letter, his/her personal address will be shown either on the Instruction Sheet or on an incoming document. Personal letters should be typed on plain paper.

58 Ramsey Crescent
Chelmsford
Essex
CM5 0GH

← sender's personal address (name is unnecessary)

DA/ST

15 June 19--

Mrs Joanna Cooper
42 Aston Glen
Pontefract
Yorkshire
LS21 9JT

← similar layout to business letter

Dear Joanna

I was so pleased to meet Tony again at the Training Exhibition in Birmingham last week and delighted to hear of the recent birth of your second son, Joshua. Please accept my sincere congratulations to you both.

I have very fond memories of the time we all spent at Sheffield University. Just this weekend I found some old photographs of the many weekend parties which we held at the house we all shared. Was it all really 12 years ago?

When I spoke to Tony I mentioned that Louise and I may be coming up to Yorkshire next month. As soon as our arrangements are finalised, I will telephone you to make some arrangements to meet. We are both looking forward to seeing you again, and to meeting the newcomer to the family.

With best wishes

Yours sincerely

DOUGLAS ALLEN

Fax message

It is becoming increasingly popular to use the facsimile machine to transmit
business correspondence. Many companies have a standard form on which
all the necessary details can be completed. Some companies prefer to use
standard business letter format for faxes, with the addition of "BY FAX"
and the fax number at the top. Any appropriate method would be
acceptable in the examination, as long as all relevant details were included.
If a fax form is used in the examination, it should be printed on
letterheaded paper and details provided as shown.

Comlon International plc

Comlon House West Street London SW1Y 2AR

tel: 0181 302 0261
telex: Comlond 888941   telemessages: Comlond London SW1   fax: 0181 302 4169

FAX MESSAGE

To	Michael Daniels, Regional Manager
Company	Comlon International (Asia) Ltd
Fax No	00 65 4785746
From	Douglas Allen, Director, Seminars and Conferences
Date	15 June 19--
No of Pages	2

← include all headings as shown

← number of pages being transmitted

← subject heading

VISIT TO SINGAPORE/MALAYSIA

Charles Lee from Sapphire Training Enterprises has invited me to chair the 10th Annual
Malaysian Secretaries Conference at the Supreme International Hotel in Kuala Lumpur.
Although this is short notice, I felt I must accept as their original Chairman has been
taken ill very suddenly.

I have therefore rearranged my schedule so that I spend 2 days in Malaysia before flying
to Singapore on Monday 14 August. My flights are now confirmed and a copy of my
itinerary is enclosed.

I hope all the arrangements for the Regional Conference are going smoothly. Please let
me have a copy of the confirmed programme as soon as possible, together with a list of
materials you want me to bring from London.

DA/ST

Memorandum

Some companies have pre-printed forms for internal memos, but in the examination you should type memos on plain paper.

MEMORANDUM

To   Todd Sutcliffe, Conference Manager

From   Douglas Allen, Director, Seminars and Conferences   ← include headings as indicated

Ref   DA/ST

Date   15 June 19--

AURORA INTERNATIONAL GROUP CONFERENCE   ← compose a relevant heading

I have now received confirmation from Aurora International that they would like us to arrange their Group Conference in December. As we have discussed, I should like you to co-ordinate all arrangements for this conference.

Obviously an appropriate venue must be found in the Leeds/Harrogate area, and you will be obtaining estimates from various hotels. However, I met the Manager of the Goodison Hotel in Leeds last week, and have subsequently written to enquire about their conference accommodation. A copy of my letter is attached and as soon as I receive a reply I will forward it to you.

I know you appreciate the importance of securing this contract with an organisation as well-known as Aurora. I feel sure you will take every step to ensure its success.

Please keep me fully informed and let me know if I can help.

Enc   ← Enc or Encs

Alternatively, a 2-column format may be preferred.

MEMORANDUM

To	Todd Sutcliffe Conference Manager	Ref	DA/ST
From	Douglas Allen Director, Seminars and Conferences	Date	15 June 19--

---

Continuation Sheet for Business Letter, Personal Letter, Fax message and Memorandum

Certain details are needed at the top of continuation sheets just in case the first page becomes detached. Although letterheaded paper has been used for the first page, continuation sheets should be typed on plain paper.

2

DA/ST

15 June 19--

Mr Anthony Maddison

← show page number, reference, date and name of addressee

We can discuss your requirements in further detail when you visit our London office at 1100 next Tuesday 15 June. Our Conference Manager, Mr Tom Sutcliffe, will be joining us and after our meeting we would be pleased if you would join us for lunch.

I look forward to meeting you again.

Yours sincerely

DOUGLAS ALLEN
Director
Seminars and Conferences

Copy to Mr Tom Sutcliffe, Conference Manager

Advertisement

You may be required to design an advertisement or a notice, the main aim of which is to attract attention. Therefore include all the relevant information in the most attractive and effective way.

Comlon Seminars and Conferences

**PERSONAL ASSISTANT
TO THE CHIEF EXECUTIVE**

Are you Capable? Competent? Committed?

This is an excellent opportunity for an experienced individual
to join a highly successful international training organisation.

You will have: - first-class communication skills
- confidence, initiative and a well-organised approach
- an operating knowledge of Word for Windows,
Excel, DBase and electronic mailing
- LCCIEB PSC or (preferably) PESD

In return we offer an excellent salary and working conditions
plus an attractive benefits package

Please send full Curriculum Vitae to

Mr Daniel Clifton, Recruitment Officer
Comlon Seminars and Conferences
Comlon House, West Street, London SW1Y 2AR

Closing Date: 21 July 19--

DA/ST
15 June 19--

← give prominence to special items as necessary or as equipment permits

← emphasise items in a variety of ways, eg emboldening, capitals, bullet points, etc

← use initiative to ensure all essential details are included

← reference/date

Job description

A job description normally gives details of the duties and responsibilities involved in the job, any supervisory duties or authority and any specific features of the post. Type a job description on plain paper, and use your initiative to display the information in the most appropriate way.

COMLON INTERNATIONAL plc

JOB DESCRIPTION

← company's name and main heading

Job Title	Personal Assistant to the Chief Executive
Division/Location	Comlon Seminars and Conferences
Reporting to	Chief Executive
Supervision/Authority	Clerical Assistant
Job Summary	To help the Chief Executive to co-ordinate his work in order to maintain the Company's high standards of quality and service

← use appropriate headings relevant to the post

Main Duties and Responsibilities

← list main duties and responsibilities

1 To deal with the Chief Executive's correspondence and take appropriate action

2 To take dictation and transcribe a variety of correspondence and documents

3 To co-ordinate appointments and maintain an efficient diary for the Chief Executive

4 To plan and co-ordinate all executive meetings and ensure accurate minutes

5 To make travel and accommodation arrangements for the Chief Executive

6 To help arrange and co-ordinate special projects when required

7 To undertake special research and collate material for inclusion in reports

8 To maintain appropriate forward planners, schedules and files

9 To supervise a Clerical Assistant and delegate appropriate duties

10 To ensure security of the office and strict confidentiality at all times

← align tens and units

DA/ST
15 June 19--

← reference/date

Invitation and Reply

Invitations are normally printed on good quality paper or card but in the examination you should use plain A4 paper.

<table>
<tr><td>

The Directors of
Excel Enterprises (Singapore)
have pleasure in inviting

....

to attend their
Centenary Celebrations
at 1400 on Tuesday 15 August 19--
at the
Prince Regent Hotel
Orchard Road

RSVP

Excel Enterprises (Singapore) Pte Ltd
25 Liang Road
#09-01 Liang Towers   DA/ST
Singapore 0922   25 June 19--

</td><td>

← display information attractively, using spacing to give prominence where necessary

← use initiative to include all relevant details

← include sender's name and address and also RSVP (meaning "Please reply")

← reference/date

</td></tr>
</table>

You may also be shown an invitation which has been received by your employer, and asked to compose an appropriate reply.

<table>
<tr><td>

Douglas Allen
Director of Comlon Seminars and Conferences

thanks

Excel Enterprises (Singapore)

for their kind invitation to their
Centenary Celebrations
on
Tuesday 15 August 19--

and has much pleasure in accepting

Comlon International plc
Comlon House
West Street
London   DA/ST
SW1Y 2AR   15 June 19--

</td><td>

← reply in a similar format to the invitation received

← show address of sender

← reference/date

</td></tr>
</table>

23

Notice and Agenda

The notice part of this document should give details of the type of meeting to be held, as well as where and when it will take place. The agenda is a list of the topics to be discussed at the meeting. The notice and agenda is normally issued by the meeting secretary and is typed on plain paper.

COMLON INTERNATIONAL plc   ← company's name, type of meeting, venue, day, date and time

OPERATIONS MEETING

The monthly Operations Meeting of the Seminars and Conferences Division will be held in Conference Suite 2, Comlon House on Friday 23 June 19-- at 1400

AGENDA

1 Apologies for Absence

2 Minutes of Meeting held on 26 May   ← use initiative to include relevant ordinary business before any special items

3 Matters Arising from the Minutes

4 Birmingham Business Exhibition

5 Aurora International Group Conference

6 Visit to Singapore

7 Any Other Business   ← include final ordinary business

8 Date of Next Meeting

Sally Turner (Ms)
Secretary

Copies to: All Committee Members

DA/ST   ← reference/date
15 June 19--

Chairman's Agenda

The person who chairs a meeting often uses a special Chairman's Agenda on which he/she will make notes during the meeting. For this purpose, a wide right-hand margin is needed with the heading 'NOTES'. Beneath each Agenda heading, notes are added which will help the Chairman as he/she conducts the meeting.

COMLON INTERNATIONAL plc

OPERATIONS MEETING   ← similar headings to
                                                                                Notice
The monthly Operations Meeting of the Seminars and Conferences Division will be held
in Conference Suite 2, Comlon House on Friday 23 June 19-- at 1400

C H A I R M A N ' S   A G E N D A
                                            NOTES   ← head the blank right-
                                                                                hand side with the
1 Apologies for Absence   1   words 'NOTES' and
   Peter Denholme on annual leave   repeat numbers
                                                                                from left
2 Minutes of Meeting held on 26 May   2
   Amend item 5.1 - seminar fee has been
   reduced to £30.

3 Matters Arising from the Minutes   3

4 Birmingham Business Exhibition   4
   Issue report on visit 14 June and
   highlight follow-up required.   ← expand agenda items
                                                                                as appropriate
5 Aurora International Group Conference   5
   Update members on new contract (file)

6 Visit to Singapore   6
   Trip extended 2 days to chair Malaysian
   Secretaries' Conference
   Update members on itinerary (file)

7 Any Other Business   7

8 Date of Next Meeting   8
   Suggest Friday 25 August at 1400

DA/ST   ← reference/date
15 June 19--

25

Minutes of a Meeting

Minutes are a record of decisions made at the meeting and sometimes the main discussions which took place. They should be written in the past tense, third person and reported speech.

COMLON INTERNATIONAL plc

MINUTES of the monthly Operations Meeting of the Seminars and Conferences Division held in Conference Suite 2, Comlon House on Friday 23 June 19-- at 1400

PRESENT   Douglas Allen, Director (Chairman)
             Daniel Clifton, Recruitment Manager
             Malcolm Long, Chief Executive
             Lesley Sharp, Marketing Manager
             Todd Sutcliffe, Conference Manager
             Anne Taylor, Training/Consultancy Manager
             Grace Trimley, Seminar Co-ordinator

                                                          ACTION

1 APOLOGIES FOR ABSENCE

   Apologies were received from Peter Denholme, who was attending
   a training course. Grace Trimley attended the meeting on his behalf.

2 MINUTES OF MEETING HELD ON 26 MAY

   In item 5.1 the fee for the Effective Public Speaking seminar in August
   was amended to £30, after which the minutes were signed by the
   Chairman as a correct record.

3 MATTERS ARISING

   There were no matters arising.

4 BIRMINGHAM BUSINESS EXHIBITION

   DA issued his report on his visit to the Business Exhibition in Birmingham
   on 14 June. Various important contacts had been made and action was
   necessary from both PD and TS. They were requested to take the
   follow-up action indicated and report back to the next meeting.   PD/TS

5 AURORA INTERNATIONAL GROUP CONFERENCE

   DA reported on his recent visit to the head office of Aurora International
   in Harrogate when confirmation had been received that they would like
   Comlon to organise their Group Conference. Approximately 200 delegates
   from Aurora's UK and European branches were expected to attend the
   conference from 11-15 December.

   TS would be co-ordinating all arrangements for this conference, and
   would report back to the next meeting on progress on obtaining suitable
   accommodation.   TS

← heading should include similar details to Notice and Agenda

← show Chairperson's name first, and then list others present in alphabetical order

← an 'ACTION' column may be necessary

2

6 VISIT TO SINGAPORE

DA had received a call from Sapphire Training Enterprises in
Kuala Lumpur to say the Chairman of their 10th Annual
Malaysian Secretaries Conference had been taken ill.
As a result, DA would be extending his forthcoming trip
by 2 days to act as Chairman of this Conference.

A copy of DA's itinerary was circulated and discussed.
The programme for Comlon's Regional Conference in
Singapore would be sent to all members as soon as it
was received from Michael Daniels.   DA

7 ANY OTHER BUSINESS

7.1   LS circulated a copy of a press release announcing the
Aurora contract. This was approved for immediate release.   LS

7.2   DC circulated a copy of an advertisement and Job Description
regarding the post of Personal Assistant to the Chief Executive.
These were approved by ML and DC was requested to proceed
with advertising immediately.   DC

8 DATE OF NEXT MEETING

It was agreed that the next meeting would be held on Friday
25 August at 1400.

....
Chairman   ← leave a space for the
                                                                         Chairman to sign
....   and date
Date

DA/ST   ← reference/date
24 June 19--

Press Release

Issuing an announcement to the press or other media about anything a company considers to be newsworthy can be a good way of obtaining publicity. It should be presented on a letterheaded paper in double spacing so that an editor can make any revisions. The most important details should be mentioned first just in case the press release is cut.

If the press release is longer than 2 pages, type '–more–' at the end of the first page, and remember to include continuation sheet details at the head of the second page.

Comlon International plc

Comlon House West Street London SW1Y 2AR

tel: 0181 302 0261
telex: Comlond 888941   telemessages: Comlond London SW1   fax: 0181 302 4169

RM/ST   ← dictator/typist reference

15 June 19--   ← date of issue

PUBLICATION DATE: Immediate   ← embargo date

NEW JOBS IN COMLON SUPERSTORE   ← appropriate headline

More than 30 new jobs could be created in Sheffield thanks to Comlon Office Supplies superstore chain.

The group - a division of Comlon International plc - already has one store in Rotherham and only last week announced plans to open new superstores in Leeds and York. Now a   ← double spacing
deal has been signed with developers Greenrows for another new Yorkshire store, on a two-acre site near Meadowhall, Sheffield.

Work has already started work on the 30,000 sq ft Sheffield superstore which should be completed later this year.   Talks are already being held with a number of potential occupiers of the rest of the site, which could include a pub, a restaurant and a major departmental store.

Ryan Mitchell, a spokesman for Comlon, today said: "We are delighted to be in a position to create new jobs in the Sheffield area, and feel confident that this new project is set to be an overwhelming success."

- ends -   ← indicate 'ends'

Contact: Ryan Mitchell, Director   ← contact name
Comlon Superstores   and details
Telephone: 0181 302 0261 (extension 267)

Itinerary

An itinerary gives full details of a journey in order of date. It shows all travel arrangements, accommodation, appointments, etc. For ease of reference all the relevant details would normally be shown on one page with appropriate sub-headings.

COMLON INTERNATIONAL plc

MR DOUGLAS ALLEN
TOUR OF MALAYSIA AND SINGAPORE
11-19 AUGUST 19--

   ← name of traveller, place/region being visited and duration of trip

FRIDAY 11 AUGUST

1045   Depart London Heathrow (BA 011)

SATURDAY 12 AUGUST

   ← sub-headings show days/dates

0930   Arrive Kuala Lumpur
             Accommodation: Supreme International, Petaling Jaya

SUNDAY 13 AUGUST

1000-1600   10th Annual Malaysian Secretaries Conference

1930   Dinner with Mr Charles Lee, Sapphire Training Enterprises Sdn Bhd

MONDAY 14 AUGUST

1150   Depart Kuala Lumpur
1240   Arrive Singapore
             Meet Michael Daniels at airport
             Accommodation: Supreme International

   ← under each date display all information clearly, perhaps in a 2/3 column format as relevant

1630   Mr Eric Wong, Excalibur Consulting Ltd

TUESDAY 15 AUGUST

1700   Centenary Celebrations, Excel Enterprises (Singapore)

WEDNESDAY 16 AUGUST

1000-1600   Comlon International (Asia) Regional Conference

FRIDAY 18 AUGUST

2330   Depart Singapore Changi International (BA 012)

SATURDAY 19 AUGUST

0755   Arrive London Heathrow

DA/ST
15 June 19--

   ← reference/date

Forms

If you are required to design a form, remember to use the space on
the paper effectively. Forms should be simple to complete and should
include all essential information. Spaces left for completion should usually
be double spaced.

COMLON SEMINARS AND CONFERENCES

EFFECTIVE PUBLIC SPEAKING SEMINAR
SATURDAY 30 AUGUST 19--

Please enrol .... representatives on this seminar. Delegates will be as follows:
(please use capitals)

NAME   DESIGNATION

....

....

....

....
(Continue overleaf if necessary)

Our cheque for £........ (£30 per person) is enclosed (payable to "Comlon Seminars and
Conferences").

Signed .... Date ....

Name (in caps) .... Title ....

Company ....

Address ....

....

Telephone Number .... Extension ....

Please return to by 30 June 19-- to   Mr Douglas Allen
                                        Director
                                        Comlon Seminars and Conferences
                                        Comlon House
                                        West Street
                                        London
                                        SW1Y 2AR

DA/ST
2 May 19--

← appropriate headings

← sufficient space
ie double line spacing
left for handwritten
completion of
necessary information

← space for signature/date
plus other relevant
details about the person
completing the form

← dots or underscore
ending at the
same point

← A date by which form
should be returned,
plus full name and
address for reply

Part C

Manuscript transcription: a workbook

The Manuscript Transcription examination tests your transcription ability in a realistic, practical office situation. A common theme and vocabulary will be used. You will notice connections between many of the documents. For example, you may be replying to an incoming letter and then sending an internal memo regarding the same matter. There may also be other documents concerning the same topic. This makes the examination very realistic and practical.

Before attempting a complete examination paper, study the method by which instructions may be given to you. These methods are explained in Unit 3. Work through this unit so that you develop the skills required and build up your production rate. After attempting a variety of assignments from each of the individual input methods you will feel more confident to move on to the complete examination papers in Part D.

Unit 3

Examination components

By the end of this unit you will:

- *be familiar with the various methods by which instructions may be given to you for composition of business communications*

- *recognise why penalty marks may be deducted*

- *appreciate the importance of using initiative to interpret the employer's written instructions*

- *be able to compose acceptable communications and display such communications in an appropriate format*

Individual input methods

Assignments in the Manuscript Transcription examination are not like those in a traditional typewriting examination. In this examination different skills are required. You must use your initiative to interpret your employer's instructions. You must choose appropriate document formats. You must compose communications which accurately convey your employer's meaning.

Assignments in this examination are based on the methods by which employers would pass on work to you in the office. These methods are:

- Composition from manuscript notes
- Replies to incoming correspondence
- Corrected typescript
- Corrected manuscript
- Special assignments

Composition from manuscript notes

Brief instructions are written down and you are required to compose the necessary document. Note that the employer is 'speaking' to *you*, instructing you what to include in the body of the message, eg 'Thank her'. 'Tell her', 'Send her', etc.

Memo to Mr Maureen Taylor

Thank her for her interesting contribution on the history of chocolate. Tell her I should like to use it for our special Centenary edition. I have made some amendments – send her an amended copy and ask her to have lunch with me next week – 16 or 17 Dec are clear but after Christmas will do if she prefers as we shall not print the centenary edition until June. Ask her to let you know which dates are convenient for her.

Replies to incoming correspondence

When a letter, memo, fax, etc is received by the employer, a few notes may be written on the document itself and you will be expected to compose an appropriate reply.

GMB ENGINEERING PLC
Units 12-16, 23 Tower Industrial Estate, Nottingham NG2 3JT
Telephone 475617   Fax 493847

IJ/FR

1 June 19--

Mr Patrick Thompson
Operations Director, Comlon Hotels
Comlon International plc
Comlon House
West Street
LONDON SW1Y 2AR

> Please reply to this letter.
> Make the points shown below.

Dear Mr Thompson

I was one of the delegates at the Businessman's Conference in Bedford last month, and I particularly enjoyed your presentation.

Our company is organising a 2-day seminar for approximately 250 administrative staff from branches throughout the UK and Europe. This will be held at the Mossbrook Hotel in Nottingham on 15/16 August. Unfortunately one of our speakers has let us down and we need someone to give a presentation on the subject of Human Relationships at Work. I realise this is very short notice, but I do hope you will be able to help us. This presentation is scheduled from 1100 to 1230 on Thursday 15 August but if this timing is inconvenient for you, we could try to rearrange our schedule. Of course we would reimburse you with our standard fee of £100 as well as covering your travel expenses.

I know our staff would be very interested to hear you speak, and do hope you will be able to participate in our seminar.

I look forward to hearing from you soon.

Yours sincerely

LORETTA JONES (Mrs)
Training and Development Manager

> - Thank
> - Happy to accept invitation. Date + time OK.
> - I have a 20 min film which I'm sure delegates will find interesting - need projector. Flip chart also useful.
> - Not familiar with Nottingham area - would appreciate map showing direction to venue.

Corrected typescript

The employer may already have some notes which have been edited. Various corrections will have been made, incorporating printers' correction signs, and you will be required to type a corrected version.

INTRODUCTION TO POLESDEN LACEY   by   S J Shepherd

The house is beautifully situated on high ground, with a fine view from the

south terrace across the park-like landscape to the Ranmore Woods on the far

side of the valley. Beyond the woods on the skyline lies Ranmore Common, well

known to walkers, while to the east above Burford Bridge are the steep slopes

of Box Hill.

The present mansion was begun in 1824 by Joseph Bonsor to the designs of

Thomas Cubitt. Surrounding an open central courtyard It is a pleasant low

building of two storeys, the walls roughcast and yellow washed but without

architectural pretensions. Though the interior of the house has been entirely

reconstructed since it was built, the exterior has been less altered and

preserves something of its Regency villa flavour. The south front with its

Ionic colonnade is apart from an extension eastwards to provide a suite of

private rooms, much as it was when first erected. It is the east front which

has undergone the greatest changes. A cupola was added and, at the entrance,

Joseph Bonsor's Doric portico was taken down and the columns re-erected in the

form of a screen at the far end of the Long Walk. It is through a new

entrance, built for Sir Clinton Dawkins, that the visitor enters today. The

house was damaged by fire in 1960 but re-opened in 1962 after careful

restoration.

provide a suite of private rooms.

Corrected manuscript

Handwritten notes may be prepared but amended, again using printers' correction signs, and you will be required to type a corrected version.

RECOMMENDED LOW PRICE HOTELS

ITALY

ROME   Hotel Windsor, Via Magna Grecia
Central, near St John's in Laterano
56 rooms all with bath/shower, aircon,
telephone, radio, colour TV. Panoramic views of
~~of the city.~~ city.

MILAN   Hotel Irma, Via Lepetit
Central, near Duomo - 52 rooms all with
private facilities, [aircon] telephone, ~~colour~~ [radio] TV. Some
rooms have balconies.

SWITZERLAND - GENEVA - Hotel Mont Blanc,
Avenue de Frontenex. Quiet position, 5 minutes
from lake and city centre 49 rooms, all
with [usual facilities] ~~bath, telephone, TV~~ some with balcony.

GERMANY - MUNICH - HOTEL PARK Schillerstrasse
[Central] ~~Downtown~~, near station. 50 rooms all with
bath, telephone, TV and minibar. Comfortable but
could be noisy. Recommended for night stops only.

LAUSANNE - Hotel Beau Rivage, Avenue de Cour,
Overlooking Lake Geneva 50 rooms with
usual facilities and mini-bar. Completely
renovated /1990. Some rooms with balconies or superb
views of the lake (Note: Roadside rooms can be noisy).

Rates at all these hotels come within our 'C' band
& charges include continental breakfast. ~~All rooms~~
~~are doubles; supplements are charged for single~~
~~occupancy & balcony rooms~~

Special assignments

Apart from general correspondence such as letters, memos and fax messages, there may be special documents to produce. Instructions for such documents will be handwritten and you will be expected to interpret the employer's requirements, produce the document and display it appropriately.

MEMORANDUM

TO   CUSTOMER RELATIONS MANAGER   DATE

FROM   ADVERTISING MANAGER

DIAMOND JUBILEE NAME COMPETITION

The Company will launch a new drinking chocolate in 1994. So far this product
has no name and, as a contribution to the Diamond Jubilee celebrations, the
Advertising Executive Committee has decided to organise an interdepartmental
competition. The aim of the competition is to find a descriptive name which
will be marketable and easy to advertise.

Please inform all members of your staff. I enclose a supply of entry forms;
additional copies can be photocopied or obtained from this department. To
facilitate administration please ask entrants to use only the official entry
form.

I give below some details of the new product which may be useful to entrants
for the competition.

The new drinking chocolate is sure to go down well with anyone who enjoys that
special Comlon chocolate taste. It suits the busy lifestyle of these days
because it is so quick and easy to make. Just pour the drink into a mug and
heat in a micro-wave for one minute - no mess,and no fuss! What is more, this
drinking chocolate is made with semi-skimmed milk so users need not feel guilty
about putting on weight. They can put up their feet and relax, enjoying its
delicious taste. This new product will be available from most supermarkets
from early 1994.

Please type a notice for the departmental noticeboard calling attention to the competition & giving details. Ask entrants to collect entry forms from you.

Check copies are on pages 171 to 175 for all these assignments.

Note: A full list of printers' correction signs which may appear in the examination is shown on page 194.

Practical work

Guidelines are now provided about each of the input methods. Work through each section in order to build up your production rate and accuracy. You will then feel much more confident when you attempt a complete examination paper. Each section comprises:

Example 1 (worked)

- A specimen assignment is illustrated.
- The suggested approach to the assignment is discussed.
- The examiner's check copy is then shown, with notes regarding specific requirements.
- A candidate's marked answer is then illustrated, and comments made regarding all the deductions under the two categories 'Display' and 'Transcription'.

Example 2 (analysis)

- A similar assignment is illustrated with guidelines regarding transcription.
- A candidate's marked answer is shown with specific comments regarding penalties for errors. These comments are categorised under 'Display' and 'Transcription'.
- After studying these comments, you should then be able to produce an accurate transcription of the assignment.

Transcription tips

The transcription tips will recap the points you have learned so far. Study them carefully before moving on to the practical assignments in each section. You may find it helpful to refer back to these tips occasionally.

Practical assignments

You are now given an opportunity to work through a variety of assignments requiring similar skills. Pointers are given to help you in transcribing each assignment.

In the actual examination you will be expected to refer to the Instruction Sheet for names, designations, addresses, etc, and perhaps to refer to other assignments for some additional details. For the purpose of working through this unit, any information you need is shown at the beginning of the assignment. The date of the examination is also shown so that you can use this when transcribing the assignment.

In the examination you will be instructed as to how your employer likes letters to be completed. In working through this unit, use upper case for the employer's name, showing courtesy title and the designation with initial capitals and lower case, eg

NERISSA LEE (Mrs)   IMRAN PATEL
Area Manager   General Manager

3.1 Composition from manuscript notes

EXAMPLE 1 (worked)

You are secretary to Mrs Rachel Thaxton, Secretarial Services Manager of
Comlon International plc. *(SSC – 2 December 1992)*

Memo to Heads of Departments – tell them

Next induction course for sec. staff
will be held on 1 Feb
Attach programme – ask them to release
any new staff joined since 30 November
& any other staff who have not attended
such a course. I need names and by 19 Jan.
designations of those attending & also names
of those who cannot attend so that I can
put them on the next course. Remind
them that I can arrange for the dept let
have replacement staff for the day if they
let me know their requirements by 19 Jan.

As you read Mrs Thaxton's notes, remember that they are not to be typed
exactly as they appear here. They are her instructions to you stating her
requirements and giving details to be included in the body of the message.

Examination approach

- First of all ask yourself about the type of document required. In this case it is a memo, so plain paper should be used.

- Remember that all memos must include the headings Memorandum/To/From/Ref/Date and jot down the details you will type alongside these headings.

- Consider an appropriate subject heading which will give a brief indication of the topic of the memo.

- Carefully read the employer's notes, crossing out instructions like 'tell them', 'ask them', 'remind them' etc, and inserting the words which you will eventually include in the message when you type it.

- Remember who is sending and who is receiving the message.

- Choose the appropriate paper and type out your answer thoughtfully.

- Check for any errors.

Here is the same assignment after a candidate has made her own notes to help her when transcribing the memo.

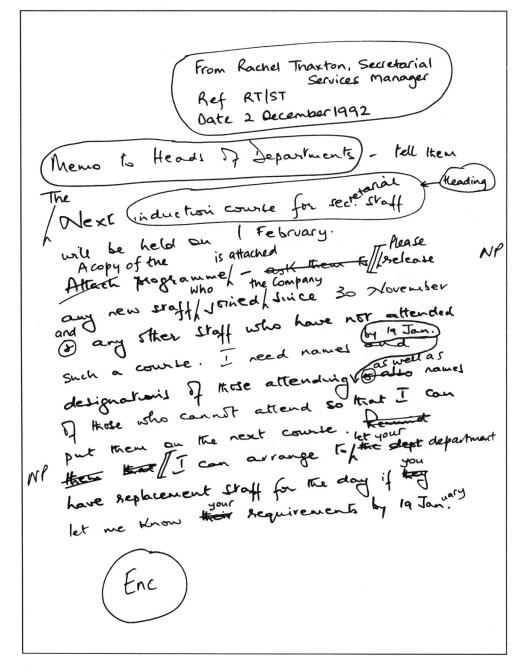

Examiner's check copy

```
M E M O R A N D U M

To     Heads of Departments

From   Rachel Thaxton, Secretarial Services Manager

Ref    RT/ST

Date   2 December 1992


INDUCTION COURSES FOR SECRETARIAL STAFF

The next induction course for secretarial staff will be held
on 1 February.  A copy of the programme is attached.

Please release any new staff who joined the Company since
30 November and any other staff who have not attended such a
course.

I need names and designations of those attending by
19 January, as well as names of those who cannot attend so
that I can put them on the next course.

I can let your department have replacement staff for the day
of the induction course if you let me know your requirements
by 19 January.




Enc
```

← Plain paper headed MEMORANDUM

← Headings TO/FROM/REF/DATE (including designation of sender)

← Appropriate heading

← Accurate interpretation of employer's notes

← Message broken down into suitable paragraphs

← Pronouns 'they' and 'their' changed to 'you' and 'your

← Enclosure indicated

Marked answer

MEMORANDUM

To   Heads of Departments   From   Rachel Thaxton

Date   2 December 1992   Ref   RT/PG

The
∧ Next induction course for secretarial staff will be held on   −1
1 February. (I have pleasure in attaching programme.)   −1

Please
(Would you be kind as to) release any new staff ⌐joined since ③⓪   −1 −1
November and any other staff who have not attended such a
course.   I need names and designation of (these) attending by   −1 −1
19 January and also names of those (who cannot attned) so that   −1
I can put them on the next course. (Remind them that) I can   −1
arrange to let the (dept.) have replacement staff (s) for the day   −1 −1
if (they) let me know (their) requirements by 19 January.   −1 −1

Enc   −1

Total Penalties = 13

Display

1 Unequal space has been left after To/Date and From/Ref. Although this has not been penalised, it is not attractive.

2 A title should have been shown for Mrs Thaxton, although again this has not been penalised here.

3 A heading should be composed, but as the topic of the memo is clearly mentioned in paragraph one, this has not been penalised.

4 After a short first paragraph, the second paragraph is too long, but again the examiner has not penalised this. (Examiners are often very lenient!)

5 The enclosure should have been indicated.

Transcription

1 'I have pleasure in attaching' and 'Would you be so kind as to release' are unnecessarily long phrases. Be brief, and come straight to the point with 'I attach' and 'Please release'.

2 The candidate has just copied the employer's simple notes, but they often need expanding to make complete sentences. In this case 'who' has been omitted.

3 When word processors automatically wrap-around at the end of lines, it often happens that figures are left on the end of lines. It is a display fault to separate at a line-end a figure from the word to which it relates. This should have been corrected when checking for errors, so that the figure '30' is placed before the month.

4 The final 's' has been omitted from 'designations' and 'those' has been mistranscribed. A typographical error has been made in 'attend'.

5 'Remind them' was an instruction to the candidate, not to be transcribed.

6 Employers often use abbreviations like dept. for 'department', so this should have been typed in full.

7 There is never a final 's' in the word 'staff' but this is a common error.

8 The candidate should have changed the pronouns to read '. . . if you let me know your . . .'.

EXAMPLE 2 (Analysis)

You are secretary to Mr Paul Winter, Editor of Historic Houses, Comlon
International plc. He is one of four editors responsible to the Chief Editor,
Mr David Simmons. *(SSC – 1 December 1993)*

Pointers

Write a memo to the Chief Editor.

Say that as Vol. 2 of Historic Houses
is nearly complete I'd like to discuss
the possibility of publishing a smaller
volume (or separate books) about some
of the smaller but very interesting
properties for which there was no low cost
room. I'd like to suggest separate
volumes for different areas, eg Wales,
Scotland, Sur England and so on.
Enclose the descriptions of the houses in
Wales I have already researched
and add the list of the others I think
worth considering. Say I'll ring him
when he returns from New York to
find out if he approves so that I can
start contacting authors.

Please get this off today. The Editor
returns tomorrow & I'd like him to
have the details before I ring.

← Remember Mr Winter is 'talking' to you.

← Omit instructions to you eg 'Say that'.

← Type abbreviations in full.

← Remember verbs like 'enclose', 'add' and 'say' to tell you what to include in the message.

45

Marked answer

```
M E M O R A N D U M

To   Chief Editor  ?              From   Paul Winter  ?              ─(
Ref  ?                            Date   1 December ───?───          ─\
                                                                     ─(
                                                     Heading         ─(
As Vol○ 2 of Historic Houses is nearly complete I would like         ─(
to discuss the possibility of publishing a smaller volume (or
(seperate) books) about some of the smaller but very                 ─(
interesting properties for which there was no room.  Separate)
(lowcost) volumes for different areas, eg Wales, Scotland, SW  } ─( ─(
England and so on.

(Enclose) are descriptions of the houses in Wales.  I have    (clumsy) ─(
already researched the houses.  (I would add) the list of the        ─(
others as I think they are worth considering.
                                                                  ─( ─(─(
I will telephone (him) when (he) return(s) from New York tomorrow.
I would like you to have the details first.  Then if you             ─(
(approves) I can start contacting authors.

Kindest regards   X                                                  ─(



───────────────   X

Paul Winter

Enc                                                                  ─(


              Total Penalties = 17
```

Display

1 Names and designations should be included for sender and recipient.

2 Dictator/typist reference omitted.

3 Year omitted in date.

4 A heading should have been included.

5 'Kindest regards' is unnecessary.

6 It has been assumed that it is the candidate's house style to type a line and a repeat of the sender's name at the foot of the memo. Although this is unnecessary, it has not been penalised.

7 The enclosure has not been indicated.

Transcription

1 Abbreviations should normally be transcribed in full – in this case 'volume'.

2 'separate' is misspelt.

3 The final sentence in paragraph one is incomplete.

4 'low cost' should be two words.

5 'Enclose' should have final 'd'.

6 The first 2 sentences of paragraph 2 sound very clumsy and would be better if they were connected.

7 The candidate has misinterpreted the employer's instructions regarding enclosing the list of other houses worth considering.

8 The candidate has forgotten who is the recipient and so has confused pronouns. This has resulted in errors with verbs.

Can you do better?

Transcribe this assignment yourself and then compare your work with the check copy on page 176.

TRANSCRIPTION TIPS FOR PRACTICAL ASSIGNMENTS

Composition from manuscript notes

1   Read the entire assignment through, remembering that the employer is talking to *you*.

2   Go through the notes again, crossing out instructions like 'Thank her', 'Tell him', 'Send him' etc, and inserting any words needed for transcription.

3   Remember who is sending and who is receiving the message. Alter the pronouns 'she', 'her', 'he', etc, accordingly.

4   Write out any abbreviations in full.

5   Indicate where you will begin new paragraphs.

6   Decide on the subject heading. Jot it down or circle it.

7   If something is to be enclosed, make a large note at the foot, so that you do not forget to type 'Enc'.

8   For letters, check inside address details and decide on a suitable salutation and complimentary close.

9   For memos, jot down names and designations of sender and recipient.

10   Remember to include reference and date.

11   Choose appropriate paper and transcribe the assignment carefully, always remembering who is writing the letter and who is receiving it.

12   Check for errors.

PRACTICAL ASSIGNMENTS

1 You are secretary to Mrs Anne Richards, Conferences Manager (Administration), Comlon International plc. Mrs Cosima Raymond is Marketing and Advertising Manager. *(SSC – 9 June 1993)*

Please type a memo to Cosima Raymond.

Thank her for letting me have a copy of her draft of the first page of the booklet she is producing for the new Edinburgh Conference Centre. Tell her I should like to use some of the information in a /handout and I have adapted her draft for this purpose. Have I her permission to use the material ~~information~~ in this form? I shall welcome her comments & suggestions. Perhaps she would like to ring me to discuss the matter.

Then type the revised publicity material and enclose a copy with the memo.

Pointers

← Memo? What paper will you use? Refer back to Specimen Document Formats and include all essential details.

← Change pronouns – say 'Thank you . . .' '. . . you are producing . . .'.

← What is the topic of the memo? Use this as the heading.

← Instead of 'Have I her permission . . .' say 'May I have your permission . . .'.

← The 'revised publicity material' mentioned at the bottom is the draft mentioned here – simply add 'A copy is enclosed' at the appropriate point.

← Remember to include 'Enc'.

2 You are secretary to Mrs Jane Harris, Advertising and Market Support, Comlon International plc. Mr Paul King is Marketing and Public Relations Director.
(PSC – 15 June 1993)
NB: The list of suggestions mentioned are suggestions for publicity and promotion aimed at young people.

Pointers

Send a memo to Mr King — heading — Caps Advertising projects for new franchises. Tell him I have some ideas I should like to discuss with him for advertising and promoting the new franchises — the ones offering fish as their speciality food. When I visited America recently I was interested to find that a large proportion of the customers for fast food was made up of children I think we shd bear this in mind when considering publicity for new outlets here.

between 5 and 12 years of age.

Type the list of suggestions I have written out o enclose it with the memo.

← Choose suitable paper and remember headings MEMORANDUM/TO/ FROM/REF/DATE.

← Change pronouns in this first sentence, and instead of saying '– the ones offering' say 'which offer'.

← Type out this abbreviation in full, ie 'should'.

← This is an instruction to you. Start your final paragraph 'I enclose a list of . . .'. Remember to include 'Enc'.

3 You are secretary to Mrs Barbara Ashton, Marketing Development Manager, Conlon International plc. Mrs Ashton leaves on 6 September on a market development trip to South East Asia. She has written separately to Best Foods (Singapore) Inc. *(PSC – 15 June 1994)*

Pointers

Please send a memo to Frances Kelly. Enclose a photocopy of my draft itinerary. Explain that I'm still awaiting replies from various government departments in the countries which I'm visiting. Also that I've written to Simon Porter, Marketing Manager, Best Foods etc — I met him recently on a management training course. I hope he will be able to provide me with some other contacts/ & further information about local laws as he has been in Singapore for ~~more than~~ six months.

I will keep her informed of my progress.

← Expand the first sentence so that it is quite clear what is being enclosed.

← Rephrase this sentence so that you do not start a sentence with 'Also', and try to avoid including a hyphen as shown in the notes.

← Expand all abbreviations, also the full company name of Best Foods.

← Remember who is writing to whom – the pronoun 'he' refers to Simon Porter.

← Here, the pronoun 'her' refers to Frances Kelly.

Notes

1 Are you remembering to include proper headings on memos? This includes full name and title for both sender and recipient, as well as the reference and date.

2 Remember that all memos should include an appropriate heading. For a heading for this memo, see the general printed instructions at the head of the assignment.

3 Remember to structure your memos correctly, and to use appropriate paragraphing.

4 Are you remembering to include 'Enc' at the end of memos when necessary? Make a note on the assignment if it will help you to remember.

4 You are secretary to Mr Paul Winter, Editor, Historic Houses, Comlon
International plc. The address of Mr S J Shepherd is Vyne Cottage, Sherborne St
John, Basingstoke, RG26 5DX. *(SSC – 1 December 1993)*

Pointers

Letter to Mr S J Shepherd
VOLUME 2 – TREASURES OF HISTORIC HOUSES –
POLESDEN LACEY

Please acknowledge receipt of
Mr Shepherd's manuscript –
congratulate him on meeting his
deadline – very rare with authors!
As it has been difficult to include
all the information we'd like to
publish (I explained on the 'phone
we're limited by production costs) I've
had to edit substantially. I hope
he doesn't think this detracts from
the value of his work.
Send him the suggested amendments
for the introduction and the re-designed
arrangements of the Italian majolica
plates. Suggest we meet for lunch to
discuss my proposals when he has had
time to consider them. Ask him to
ring you. Tell him I agree his spelling
~~of majolica~~ is correct but we have
decided to use the anglicised form –
MAJOLICA – throughout the book.

← You are told to 'Please acknowledge . . .' so simply say 'Thank you for . . . and congratulations . . .'.

← Dashes are often used when hand-writing notes, but try to avoid using dashes in your transcript.

← Begin a second paragraph 'As I explained on the telephone . . .'.

← Consider the context. Perhaps 'Therefore' will be useful?

← 'Send him'? Say 'I enclose'.

← This section should be restructured. Use one paragraph on the topic of 'Italian majolica' and start a final paragraph with 'When you have had time to consider my proposals . . .'.

← 'Ask him to ring you.' Who does 'you' refer to?

Notes

1 This time you have to prepare a letter. Choose correct paper and remember the preliminary items: reference, date and full inside address.

2 Your employer refers to 'Mr Shepherd' in his notes, so use this in the salutation. Remember that your complimentary close must match, ie 'Yours sincerely'.

3 Study the notes carefully. It would be a good idea to go through them crossing out instructions like 'Please acknowledge . . .' and writing in what you will actually transcribe, ie 'Thank you for . . .'.

4 Consider appropriate structure and paragraphing. In this letter, the final paragraph cannot simply be copied; it needs careful rephrasing.

5 Remember as you are making notes on your copy of this assignment, write 'Enc' at the foot so that you do not omit this at the end of your letter.

5 You are secretary to Mark Davidson, Manager, Advertising and Marketing Department, Comlon International plc. Mr Davidson has been invited by The London Toy Retail Trade Association to be the Guest Speaker at their Annual Luncheon on 17 November. Mr James Buckenham is Chairman and Chief Executive. *(SSC – 8 June 1994)*

Pointers

Write a memo to Mr Buckenham (he's away until 15 June)

Tell him about the invitation from The London Toy Retail Trade Association and enclose a photocopy of my reply and my suggested headlines for my speech. Ask him to let me know if he sanctions my acceptance – perhaps his secretary would telephone you so that you can date and send out my acceptance letter. Ask him to let me know if he would like to make any suggestions for my talk. Also enclose my proposed advertisement for to introduce our new range of creative toys. Perhaps we could use something like this as a flier to build up to a national TV and newspaper campaign for December.

← Instead of 'Tell him about . . .' say 'I have received an invitation . . .' and give full details.

← Mr Davidson wants to know two things: if Mr Buckenham sanctions (approves) his acceptance of the invitation and if he would like to make any suggestions for Mr Davidson's talk. Put both these points together.

← The advertisement for creative toys is a separate issue so use two separate subheadings.

Notes

1 Another memo this time. Choose correct paper and remember to include all the details opposite TO/FROM/REF/DATE.

2 If you read the notes carefully you will realise that the memo refers to two separate topics – an invitation and also an advertisement. Consider using two separate headings, or even numbered points.

3 Remember again that these are your employer's rough jottings. You will need to rephrase some sentences and use appropriate language.

4 Consider appropriate structure when planning your transcription.

5 Once again, several documents are enclosed, so make a note on the assignment to remind you not to forget 'Encs'.

3.2 Replies to incoming correspondence

EXAMPLE I (worked)

You are secretary to Mrs Margaret Johnson, Manager of Customer Relations at Comlon Chocolates. *(PSC – 15 June 1992)*

An enquiry has been received from Fiona Wilson, a schoolgirl, who wants information about chocolate for her school project. Mrs Johnson has written some notes on the incoming letter and you have to compose a suitable reply.

Examination approach

- Read the incoming letter carefully, considering the reply which the writer is expecting.

- Read the employer's instructions telling you how to reply to the letter. Look specifically for the verbs like 'acknowledge', 'suggest' and 'include' which tell you what to incorporate in the message.

- Draft the parts of the reply which you are required to compose – in this case just the opening and closing sections. The printed information about chocolate will simply need to be copied.

- Check that your reply is structured logically and remember to paragraph.

- Consider the 'mechanical details', ie paper to be used, reference and date, inside address, salutation, complimentary close, etc.

- Choose the appropriate paper and type out your answer thoughtfully.

- Check for errors.

Examiner's check copy

Comlon International plc

Comlon House West Street London SW1Y 2AR

tel: 0181 302 0261
telex: Comlond 888941   telemessages: Comlond London SW1   fax: 0181 302 4169

MJ/ST

15 June 1992

Miss Fiona Wilson
6 Church Street
Portsmouth
PO13 2LV

Dear Fiona

Thank you for your recent letter. I was interested to learn
that you have chosen chocolate as the subject for your school
project.

Chocolate is derived from the cocoa bean, which is the seed
of the cocoa fruit that grows in large pods on cocoa trees.
The bean is removed from the pod and fermented in a bacteria
solution that starts developing the flavour. After drying,
the beans are roasted, sifted to remove any stones or shells
and then ground into cocoa liquor.

Most chocolate undergoes a dutching process, where a small
amount of an alkaline substance is added to enhance the
flavour. The liquor is then pressed or put in a solvent to
remove the fat, known as cocoa butter. And because chocolate
is a vegetable product, none of this fat contains
cholesterol.

Cocoa butter is then blended with some residual cocoa powder,
other fats, emulsifiers (to make it smooth and blendable),
sweeteners (usually sugar), flavours, milk and milk products
such as whey and milk solids.

I enclose some leaflets about Comlon and its products.
I hope you will find this information useful. One of the
leaflets gives information about school visits. Perhaps you
and your school friends would like to visit our factory in
Southampton to see how Comlon confectionery is produced.
Please ask your teacher to telephone the factory at the
telephone number shown on the leaflet to make arrangements.

I hope you find this information useful and wish you success
with your project.

Yours sincerely

MARGARET JOHNSON (Mrs)
Manager
Customer Relations

. Encs

← letterheaded paper

← reference/date

← inside address copied correctly
from incoming letter, plus
correct courtesy title 'Miss'

← Appropriate salutation

← Suitable opening
paragraph

← Straight copying of
printed information
about chocolate

← Suitable closing section
following written instructions,
ie mentioning enclosed leaflets
and suggesting school visit

← Use of initiative in
suggesting teacher
telephones regarding
school visit

Marked answer

Comlon International plc

Comlon House West Street London SW1Y 2AR

tel: 0181 302 0261
telex: Comlond 888941   telemessages: Comlond London SW1   fax: 0181 302 4169

MJ/PG
15 June 1992   −1

Miss
/ Fiona Wilson
  6 Church Street
  PORTSMOUTH
  PO13 2LV

Dear (Miss Fiona)   −1

(I acknowledge receipt of) your letter which (is pass to)   −1   −1
(Customer Relations). Enclosed is (the usual information)   −1   −1 −1
(leaflet) and (you could suggest) that your school might like to
visit our Southampton factory.

Chocolate is derived from the (cocao) bean, which is the seed   −1
of the (cocao) fruit that grows in large pods on (cocao) trees.
The bean is removed from the pod and fermented in a bacteria
solution that starts developing the flavour. After drying,
the beans are (rosted), sifted to remove any stones or shells   −1
and then ground into (cocao) (ligour.)   −1

Most chocolate undergoes a (dulching) process, where a small   −1
amount of an alkaline substance is added to enhance the
flavour. The liquor is then pressed or put in a solvent to
remove the fat, known as (cocao) butter. And because chocolate
is a vegetable product, none of this fat contains (cholester-) −1
(ol.)

(Cocao) butter is then blended with some residual (cocao) powder,
other fats, (emulsfiers) (to make it smooth and blendable),   −1
sweeteners (usually sugar), flavours, milk and milk products
such as whey and milk solids.

Please let me know if you require any further information.

                              ↑
                              | ?
                              ↓

            Yours (faithfully)   −1

            MARGARET JOHNSON (Mrs)
            (Customer Relations Manager)   −1

Enc   −1   Total Penalties = 16

Display

1 Spacing is uneven between reference and date and also after the last line of the letter. Although this has not been penalised, it is not attractive.

2 A courtesy title has not been included in the inside address.

3 The incorrect salutation has been used, and the instruction sheet stated that Mrs Johnson's title should be shown as on the check copy.

4 The enclosure has not been indicated.

Transcription

1 'I acknowledge receipt of' is very old-fashioned. Simply use 'Thank you for your letter dated . . .'.

2 The candidate has misunderstood the writing at the top of the letter, obviously written in the mail room when opening this letter. The letter has subsequently been passed to the Customer Relations Department, which is why Mrs Johnson is now replying to it.

3 The final 's' has been omitted from 'leaflets', and the candidate should have said a little more about the information leaflets.

4 The employer's note has been misinterpreted. She was directing the verb 'suggest' to the candidate, not to Fiona. Again the candidate has done little more than copy the employer's notes.

5 'Cocoa' has been misspelt on every occasion. This has been penalised only once.

6 The word 'flavour' has been spelled differently to the spelling shown on the assignment ('flavor'). As both are acceptable, and as the candidate has been consistent, this has not been penalised.

7 Typographical errors have not been corrected in 'roasted', 'liquor', 'dutching' and 'emulsifiers'.

8 'Cholesterol' has been divided incorrectly. Two characters should never be left alone either at the end of one line or at the beginning of the next. Candidates are advised not to divide words which might mean a loss of marks.

EXAMPLE 2 (analysis)

You are secretary to Miss Jane Wittington, Editor of Sweet News at Comlon International plc. The Press Officer is Mr Martin Gardner. Miss Wittington has received a letter from The Westin Hotel. Read the incoming letter first, considering the expected response. Then study your employer's notes carefully. *(PSC – 9 December 1992)*

Pointers

```
                         THE WESTIN HOTEL
                          Cranbrook Road
                          SLOUGH  Berks
                            SL2 3YB

    Tel: 0753 5532296b              FAX   0753 65532297

    Ref: JS/E/12

    8 December 1992

    Miss Jane Wittington
    Editor, Sweet News
    Comlon International plc
    West Street
    London      SW1Y 2AR

    Dear Miss Wittington

    CONFERENCE FACILITIES RESERVATION - PRIZE AWARDS
```

Handwritten note: Confirm booking for 17.2.93 & facilities, also 2 double rooms for night of 16 Feb. Mr Gardner & I will call to see Mr Short 1000 7.1.93 – ask him to ring for to confirm or suggest alternative.

```
    I refer to our telephone conversation this morning regarding your requirements
    for conference facilities near London Airport for the special staff Prize Award
    ceremonies in the Comlon centenary year.

    Our proximity to the airport has made us popular with day visitors from Europe.
    I can offer you the use of conference facilities in our Princess Suite on
    Wednesday 10 or 17 February 1993. I enclose a brochure from which you will
    see that the size of the Suite should be sufficient for your requirements.  I
    can offer you a 25% discount on the prices quoted if you can let me have a
    confirmed reservation in writing by 16 December.

    When you confirm your booking please let me know whether you will need any of
    the following facilities in addition to those shown in the brochure

    1  floor microphones
    2  large screen            ✓
    3  video cassette player   ✓  VHS
    4  slide carousel          ✓
    5  overnight accommodation for delegates.  - book 2 doubles

    Our price includes morning coffee and afternoon tea.  I shall be pleased to
    discuss menus for lunch and/or dinner.  Perhaps you would like to visit us to
    see the facilities we offer.  Please let me know a date and time convenient to
    you and I shall ensure that I or one of my assistants is available to help you.

    Yours sincerely

    [signature]

    GENERAL MANAGER

    Enc
```

← The date chosen for the conference has been circled.

← The discount is underlined so it needs acknowledging in the reply.

← The facilities ticked will be required for the conference.

← This underlined point needs a response (see handwritten notes).

Marked answer

Here is one candidate's answer, with notes from the examiner.

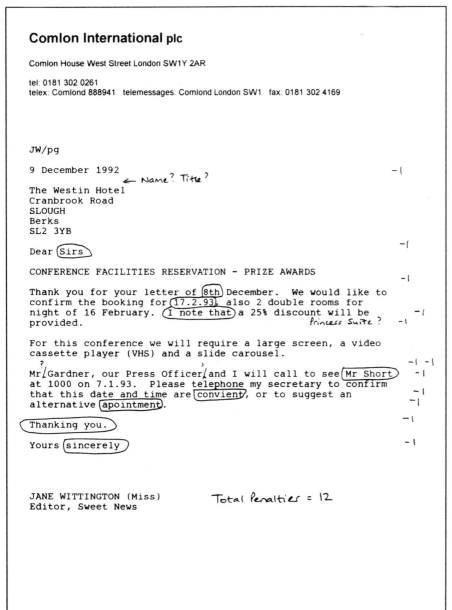

Display

1 Letterheaded paper used correctly.

2 Correct reference and date.

3 Inside address should have incorporated Mr Short's full name and title.

4 The salutation should have been 'Dear Mrs Short'.

5 Heading correctly copied from incoming letter.

6 'Yours sincerely' should not be used with 'Dear Sirs'.

Transcription

1 Dates have been displayed inconsistently.

2 No mention has been made of the facilities required, ie Princess Suite.

3 The discount has been acknowledged, but a simple 'thank you' could have been included.

4 Mr Gardner's full name should have been shown.

5 A comma is required after Press Officer.

6 The candidate has forgotten the letter is being sent to Mr Short, so the pronoun 'you' should have been used.

7 Spelling errors have been made with 'convenient' and 'appointment'.

8 It is unnecessary to close with 'Thanking you'.

9 Quite often the employer's brief notes have to be rearranged and information added to make sense of the message. In this case, the candidate has made little attempt to structure this letter logically, particularly in paragraph one.

Can you do better?

Transcribe this assignment yourself and then compare your work with the check copy on page 177.

TRANSCRIPTION TIPS FOR PRACTICAL ASSIGNMENTS

Replies to incoming correspondence

1 Note who has written the incoming letter – both the person and the company if applicable.

2 Read the incoming letter carefully, noting the structure and highlighting sections which refer to the response required.

3 Read the employer's notes, picking out verbs which tell you what to do, like 'confirm', 'ask', 'accept', 'leave', 'send', 'draw'.

4 If anything is to be enclosed, write 'Enc' at the bottom of the assignment.

5 Consider the inside address details and a suitable salutation and complimentary close.

6 Make a draft of the body of the message, remembering correct structure, paragraphing and tone.

7 Remember who is sending and who is receiving the message.

8 Check the employer's instructions again to ensure nothing has been overlooked.

9 Choose appropriate paper and transcribe the assignment carefully.

10 Check for errors.

PRACTICAL ASSIGNMENTS

1 You are secretary to Mr Mark Davidson, Manager, Advertising and Marketing Department, Comlon International plc. A copy of this letter should be marked for James Buckenham, Chairman and Chief Executive. Mr Buckenham is away until 15 June and Mr Davidson does not want to send this letter until Mr Buckenham has approved his acceptance of this invitation. *(SSC – 8 June 1994)*

THE LONDON TOY RETAIL TRADE ASSOCIATION
Cordwainers Street
London
EC4 9HY

AF/BP

1 June 1994

Mr Mark Davidson
Manager, Advertising/Marketing
Comlon International plc
West Street
LONDON   SW1Y 2AR

Dear Mr Davidson

ANNUAL LUNCHEON 1994

The annual luncheon of the London Toy Retail Trade Association will be held at the Old Ford Hotel, Stratford-le-Bow, on Thursday 17 November 1994. The President and Committee invite you to be their Guest Speaker.

The Association, which is affiliated to the BTHA, has a membership of over 600 representing retailers of toys in London and the Home Counties. It is expected that about 250 members will attend the luncheon.

The reputation of Comlon Toys is known and admired; a talk from you would be greatly appreciated. Members will be interested to hear how the Company became established and how it has maintained its high standards through two world wars and so many economic crises.

As the full impact of the single European market is felt members are becoming increasingly worried about safety standards and will welcome your suggestions and guidance.

If you are able to accept our invitation the President and Committee invite you to join them for pre-lunch aperitifs at noon in the Johnson Bar.

After the customary toasts our Guest Speaker usually has the floor from 1430 to 1500.

I sincerely hope that you will be able to accept. Please telephone me if you need more details.

Yours sincerely

David Simonson

DAVID SIMONSON
Programme Secretary

Handwritten note: Please accept & enclose copy of my suggested speech headlines. Ask him to let me know if the Association would like any other subjects included. Leave date open until we receive OK from Chief Executive.

Pointers

← Mr Davidson says 'Please accept . . .' – consider what is being accepted, and include all the relevant details in the opening paragraph.

← Start a new paragraph to enclose suggested speech headlines. Instead of 'Ask him . . .' say 'Please let me know if . . .'.

← The incoming letter uses 'Dear Mr Davidson' so the reply should begin 'Dear Mr Simonson'.

← How will you close this letter? You could refer to this paragraph and say 'I look forward to . . .'.

Notes

1 The instructions at the head of this assignment will have given you the necessary background information.

2 Read the incoming letter carefully and consider the reply which Mr David Simonson is expecting.

3 Now read the employer's notes giving instructions regarding the reply.

4 Remember to use letterheaded paper, but only type a reference at the top. Your employer asks you to 'leave the date open . . .'.

5 Address the letter appropriately using the name and title (remember 'Mr') from the foot of the letter and the company name and address from the incoming letterhead.

6 Draft the letter in manuscript first, so that you make sure it is worded and structured correctly before transcribing.

2 You are secretary to Mr Geoff Brady, Manager (Coaches), Comlon International plc. Assignment 4, mentioned in the employer's notes, was an information sheet giving details of one-day coach excursions during April and May 1994.
(PSC – 8 December 1993)

Pointers

```
                                              17 York Drive
                                              London     NW12 3YR

          1 December 1993

          The Manager (Coaches)
          Comlon International plc
          Comlon House
          West Street
          LONDON      SW1Y 2AR

          Dear Sir

          Two years ago my husband and I spent a very enjoyable weekend in Brussels on a
          leisure coach trip organised by your company.

          We have decided that we should like to take a short break in the Spring next
          year to visit the Dutch bulbfields as we have heard so much about their beauty.

          Please let me know if your company will be running coach trips to Holland in
          1994.  We are also interested in one day shopping excursions to the Continent
          and in trips to Paris EuroDisney to which we should like to take our
          grandchildren.

          Yours faithfully

          DOREEN FOSTER (Mrs)
```

Please acknowledge. Tell her that the 1994 brochure is being printed – we'll send her a copy as soon as possible. Send her a copy of Assignment 4 and draw her attention to the special excursions and the one-day coach trip to Bruges and Dunkirk.

← Compose a complete opening sentence by saying 'Thank you . . . enquiring about visits to . . .'.

← Start a new paragraph with 'Our 1994 brochure is . . . but a copy will be sent . . .'.

← Mention the information sheet being enclosed and say 'You may be particularly interested in . . .'.

Notes

1 Remember to read the incoming letter carefully and consider the reply the sender is expecting.

2 Use appropriate paper and insert appropriate preliminary details before the salutation.

3 Will the salutation be 'Dear Doreen', 'Dear Mrs Foster' or 'Dear Madam'?

4 You will need to expand the employer's notes quite considerably. Structure your reply carefully, also remembering the extra notes given at the head of the assignment.

5 Draft a reply carefully before transcribing.

3.3 Corrected typescript

EXAMPLE 1 (worked)

You are secretary to Paul Winter, Editor of Historic Houses, Comlon International plc. *(SSC – 1 December 1993)*

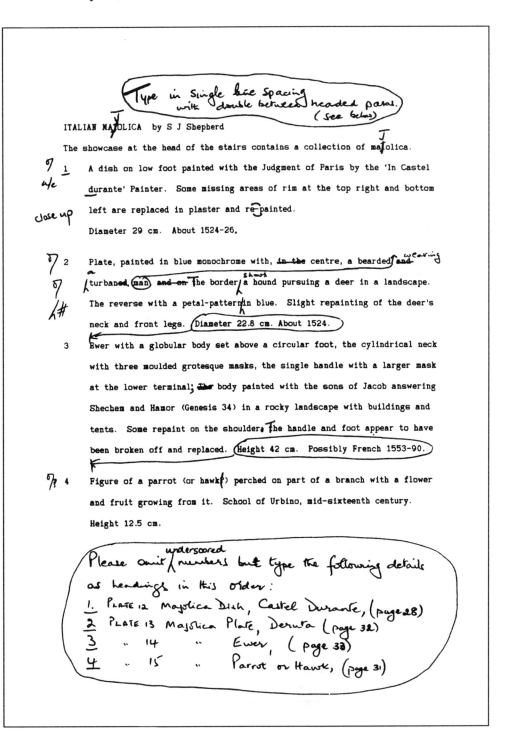

Mr Winter already has a draft of some information about Italian Majolica but he has made some amendments and asks you to retype it.

This is an exercise in interpretation so that the information is rearranged and displayed in accordance with the employer's instructions.

Examination approach

- Look for the handwritten instruction which tells you what is expected of you in this assignment. Usually, this is in a balloon at the top of the assignment, as in this case. The instruction tells you that your transcript should be in single line spacing, not double as in the original draft.

- There may be additional instructions elsewhere on the page, so look around carefully. Here the employer has written further notes at the foot of the page. These are instructions regarding an amendment to the display which tell you to omit numbers and use, instead, the headings stated.

- Look through the assignment carefully, making sure you see where each of the headings should be typed.

- Check through the printers' correction signs and decide how the amendments should be made.

- In this assignment you will notice the vocabulary is quite technical, being names and descriptions of paintings. This should tell you that you will need to take extra care when typing this assignment, and also with proofreading.

- Choose the appropriate paper and type out your answer.

- Check for errors.

Examiner's check copy

ITALIAN MAJOLICA by S J Shepherd   ← Plain paper

The showcase at the head of the stairs contains a collection
of majolica.

PLATE 12 Majolica Dish, Castel Durante, (page 28)   ← Single spacing

A dish on low foot painted with the Judgment of Paris by the
'In Castel Durante' Painter. Some missing areas of rim at
the top right and bottom left are replaced in plaster and
repainted.
Diameter 29 cm. About 1524-26.

PLATE 13 Majolica Plate, Deruta, (page 32)   ← Numbers omitted and shoulder headings inserted according to instructions

Plate, painted in blue monochrome with, centre, a bearded man
wearing a turban. The border shows a hound pursuing a deer
in a landscape. The reverse with a petal-pattern in blue.
Slight repainting of the deer's neck and front legs.
Diameter 22.8 cm. About 1524.

PLATE 14 Majolica Ewer, (page 33)   ← All printers' correction signs accurately interpreted

Ewer with a globular body set above a circular foot, the
cylindrical neck with three moulded grotesque masks, the
single handle with a larger mask at the lower terminal; body
painted with the sons of Jacob answering Shechem and Hamor
(Genesis 34) in a rocky landscape with buildings and tents.   ← Insertions correctly placed
Some repaint on the shoulder. The handle and foot appear to
have been broken off and replaced.
Height 42 cm. Possibly French 1553-90.

PLATE 15 Majolica Parrot or Hawk, (page 31)

Figure of a parrot (or hawk) perched on part of a branch with   ← Displayed as instructed
a flower and fruit growing from it. School of Urbino, mid-
sixteenth century.
Height 12.5 cm.

PW/ST
1 December 1993   ← Reference/date

Marked answer

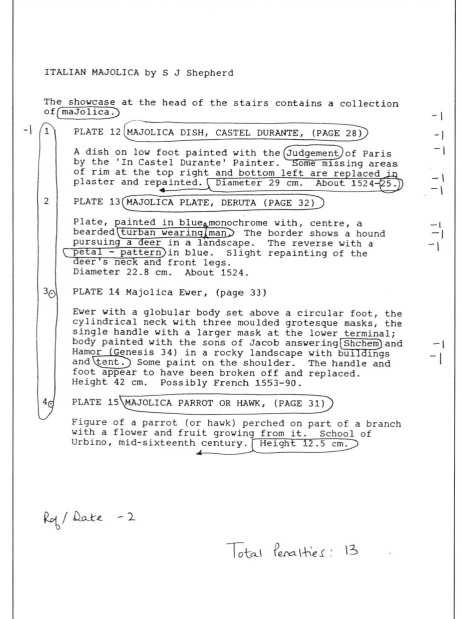

ITALIAN MAJOLICA by S J Shepherd

The showcase at the head of the stairs contains a collection of majolica.   -1

-1   1   PLATE 12 MAJOLICA DISH, CASTEL DURANTE, (PAGE 28)   -1
                                                                                   -1
            A dish on low foot painted with the Judgement of Paris
            by the 'In Castel Durante' Painter. Some missing areas
            of rim at the top right and bottom left are replaced in   -1
            plaster and repainted. Diameter 29 cm.   About 1524-25.   -1

      2   PLATE 13 MAJOLICA PLATE, DERUTA (PAGE 32)

            Plate, painted in blue monochrome with, centre, a   -1
            bearded turban wearing man The border shows a hound   -1
            pursuing a deer in a landscape. The reverse with a   -1
            petal - pattern in blue. Slight repainting of the
            deer's neck and front legs.
            Diameter 22.8 cm. About 1524.

      3   PLATE 14 Majolica Ewer, (page 33)

            Ewer with a globular body set above a circular foot, the
            cylindrical neck with three moulded grotesque masks, the
            single handle with a larger mask at the lower terminal;
            body painted with the sons of Jacob answering Shchem and   -1
            Hamor (Genesis 34) in a rocky landscape with buildings   -1
            and tent. Some paint on the shoulder. The handle and
            foot appear to have been broken off and replaced.
            Height 42 cm. Possibly French 1553-90.

      4   PLATE 15 MAJOLICA PARROT OR HAWK, (PAGE 31)

            Figure of a parrot (or hawk) perched on part of a branch
            with a flower and fruit growing from it. School of
            Urbino, mid-sixteenth century. Height 12.5 cm.

Ref / Date - 2

Total Penalties: 13

Display

1 The candidate has not followed the instruction shown at the end of the assignment. The underscored numbers should have been omitted. The candidate lost a mark for inserting the numbers. Although there is too much space after the numbers before the headings (only two spaces are necessary) this has not been penalised; the candidate has also typed numbers '1' and '2' without punctuation, but '3' and '4' with a full stop.

2 All the headings should have been typed in lower case with initial capitals and underscore as shown in the manuscript. The candidate has only displayed the third heading correctly, with the other 3 headings in upper case.

3 The final line in each section should have been displayed at the left margin. The candidate has not done this in the first or final section. It has been penalised only once.

Transcription

1 'Judgment' has been misspelled.

2 '1524–26' has been copied incorrectly.

3 The candidate has mistranscribed 'man wearing a turban', losing one mark for the transposition of 'man/turban' and one mark for omitting 'and'.

4 'petal-pattern' is hyphenated. The candidate has left a space before and after, indicating a dash.

5 'Shechem' has been misspelled.

6 The final 's' has been omitted from 'tents'.

EXAMPLE 2 (analysis)

You are secretary to Mrs Jane Harris, Advertising and Marketing Support,
Comlon International plc. *(PSC – 16 June 1993)*

NEW/FRANCHISES SPECIALISING IN FAST FOOD

(UK inserted above)

u/s SUGGESTIONS FOR PUBLICITY & PROMOTIONS ~~DIRECTED TO~~ AIMED ~~AT~~ stet
YOUNG PEOPLE (for discussion)

1 PUBLICITY – advertising in

1.1 local newspapers

1.2 local radio

l/c 1.3 National TV at children's viewing time

2 PROMOTIONS

2.1 Children's special occasion functions eg
birthday parties, end-of-term celebrations

2.3 Giveaways eg special occasion favours,
balloons, paper hats (all with a fish
motif – see below)

2.1 Competitions eg quizzes, puzzles, painting
and drawing (with prizes of free meal
vouchers to be spent at/new fast food outlets)

2.4 The creation of a comic character
designed to appeal to children. (I am
~~think~~ sure one of our artists could create
a cartoon fish, which could be incorporated in the
franchise logo design.)

2.5 The use of a cartoon character in
animated advertisements

2.6 Lucky Draws 2.7 Special discount
offers 2.8 Special children's menus.

Pointers

1 Mrs Harris has drafted a list of suggestions and you need to incorporate all the changes she has made.

2 Read the assignment first to get an idea of the theme.

3 Look at the layout and decide how you will display the information (single spacing with double between paragraphs).

4 Check all the amendments and correction signs and interpret them correctly.

5 Remember reference and date.

Marked answer

Here is one candidate's answer, with notes from the examiner.

Display

1 Plain paper has been used correctly.

2 No thought has been given to display – only part way through has the candidate decided to use double spacing between numbered items. This has resulted in a block of information which is hard to read, and has meant that the lower half of the page is blank.

3 Reference and date omitted.

NEW UK FRANCHISE SPECIALISING IN FAST FOOD   *Display -1*

SUGGESTIONS FOR PUBLICITY (&) PROMOTION AIMED AT   *-1*
YOUNG PEOPLE (for discussion)

1   PUBLICITY - advertising in   *-1*
    1.1   local newspaper
    1.2   local radio
    1.3   national TV at childrens viewing time   *-1*

2   PROMOTION   *-1*
    2.1   Competitions eg (quizes), puzzles, painting and   *-1*
      drawing (with prizes of free meal vouchers to be
      spent at/fast food outlets)   *^new*
    2.2   Children's special (occassion) function eg birthday   *-1 -1*
      parties, end-of-term-celebrations
    2.3   Giveaways eg special occasion (functions) eg balloons,   *-1*
      paper hats (all with a fish (motif-see) below)   *-1*

    2.4   The creation of a comic character designed to appeal
      to children. (I am sure one of our (artist) could   *-1*
      create a cartoon fish which/be incorporated in the   *^could -1*
      franchise logo design.)

    2.5   The use of this cartoon character in animated
      advertisement.

    2.6   Lucky Draws

    2.7   Special discount offers

    2.8   Special children's menus.

Ref/Date   -2

Total Penalties = 14

Transcription

1 The ampersand (&) has been copied – it should have been transcribed in full and written as 'and'.

2 The apostrophe has been omitted in 'children's', although correctly inserted on other occasions.

3 Typographical and spelling errors have been made in several words, although these were correctly spelled on the manuscript (newspapers, quizzes, occasion, functions, artists).

4 The word 'favours' has been mistranscribed as 'functions'.

5 Some words have been omitted through carelessness ('new', 'could').

6 The dash has been displayed incorrectly – a space is required before and after.

Can you do better?

Transcribe this assignment yourself and then compare your work with the check copy on page 178.

TRANSCRIPTION TIPS FOR PRACTICAL ASSIGNMENTS

Corrected typescript or manuscript

1 Locate the handwritten instructions telling you what is required. Instructions will usually be at the top in a balloon, but check for other instructions elsewhere.

2 Check particularly for instructions giving you specific information about display, spacing, enumeration, headings, etc.

3 Read through the assignment carefully, and as you read it imagine how it will appear when typed.

4 Check correction signs, amendments and insertions so that you interpret them correctly.

5 Keep in mind the purpose of the document and what it will be used for.

6 For memos, jot down names and designations of sender and recipient.

7 For letters, check inside address details and use a suitable salutation/complimentary close.

8 Remember to include reference and date.

9 Remember 'Enc' if appropriate.

10 Choose appropriate paper and transcribe the assignment carefully.

11 Check for errors.

PRACTICAL ASSIGNMENTS

1 You are secretary to Mrs Barbara Ashton, Marketing Development Manager, Comlon International plc. *(PSC – 15 June 1994)*

MANAGER
MRS ANN MASON, ~~DIRECTOR~~, BAKERY/DELICATESSEN DEPT

CHRISTMAS 1994 - SPECIAL PROMOTION - PARTY TIME SUGGESTIONS

~~Try to offer something to appeal to all tastes and ensure that everything has~~ The bakery and Delicatessen sections of the Comlon supermarkets have everything you need to impress your party guests.

TO CREATE AN IMPRESSIVE SPREAD

10 Arrange snacks on small plates to avoid half-empty platters.

8 Arrange the food in groups with a little of each item garnished with lettuce, herbs or spring onion.

2 Keep the menu to six or seven choices, retaining some food for replenishing plates.

4 Use cup-shaped radicchio to hold dips and sauces. Offer tortilla chips, crisps and crudités for dipping.

7 Make a lemon and cucumber twist. Sandwich a slice of cucumber between two slices of lemon, cut from outside to centre, twist in opposite directions and fan out the layers.

12 Add a slice of lemon to each cube section of the ice-maker. Top up with water and freeze to provide lemon ice for drinks.

3 Spoon prawns or smoked salmon paté into lettuce leaves.

5 Spread soft cheese on to split mini-rolls and top with smoked salmon and lemon.

6 Fill small baskets with varieties of bread in different shapes and sizes such as bread sticks, mini-rolls, garlic bread slices, Melba toast or pitta bread.

9 ~~10~~ Use round plates for circular foods such as vol au vents and mini-quiches, oblong platters for sausage rolls, cheese straws and spring rolls.

11 Arrange sweet alternatives such as tiny eclairs, choux buns and bite-sized iced and creamy delights in separate groups according to colour and shape.

13 ~~12~~ Make your party cake the centrepiece - Comlon's Bakery can provide an appropriate cake for any occasion.

1 Try to offer something to appeal to all tastes, sweet, savoury, and and ensure that everything ~~has plate appeal~~ looks inviting.

← Type very carefully, inserting the information shown in balloons in the correct place.

← There are 13 numbered points, so align the numbers correctly, ie
  8
  9
  10

© LCCI 1994

Notes

1 This assignment has been transcribed once and your employer has amended it. Study it carefully and consider the manuscript revisions.

2 Use similar layout to the original format. There are two headings in capitals, followed by an introductory sentence and then a subheading before the numbered points.

3 Transcribe this assignment carefully and do not rush it. There are some words which may be unfamiliar so take particular care.

4 Remember to include reference and date at the bottom left.

2 You are secretary to Mrs Anne Richards, Conferences Manager (Administration), Comlon International plc. You have been asked to produce a one page handout on the new Comlon Conference Centre in Edinburgh. *(SSC – 9 June 1993)*

Pointers

PRESS RELEASE   COMLON INTERNATIONAL plc

Please type material enclosed in brackets [ ] on separate lines.

EDINBURGH CONFERENCE CENTRE

Come Autumn 1993 Comlon International plc will unveil its state-of-the-art conference and exhibition facilities in Edinburgh. The new Comlon Conference Centre in Queen's Road, Edinburgh will open in September 1993.

NP The Centre includes [a large column-free exhibition hall] [12 seminar rooms] and [2 function

NP rooms] it will be The perfect venue for memorable [exhibitions] [product launches] [incentive programmes] [seminars and conferences].

← Use separate lines for these points, as instructed.

To ensure the success of your event our brigade of efficient catering staff will attend to your every need. Our versatile and experienced team of chefs will make dining a pleasure with culinary creations from our modern kitchens.

ORCHARD EXHIBITION HALL

The main hall is an impressive columnless room boasting with an area of 1234 metres sq m and accommodation, theatre-style, for 1500 persons. (1282 sq ft) and a height of 6 metres. Located on the second level, the hall can be partitioned into 3 rooms, each approx 400 sq m with individually controlled sound and light systems as well as independent retractable projection screens. The adjacent Foyer measuring 410 sq m, is ideal for delegates to meet for tea/coffee breaks. and There is a fully equipped bar for pre-lunch and dinner drinks.

FUNCTION ROOMS

← 'sq m' can be typed exactly as shown.

– each approx 60 sq m –

Two function rooms - Valencia and Apricot - are also located on the second level. These rooms each are suitable for meetings of 60 to 80 persons. or buffets for 48 persons.

← 'theatre-style' and 'pre-lunch' are hyphenated, so no space before or after the hyphens.

← There should be a space on both sides of these dashes.

Notes

1 This was originally drafted on two pages in double line spacing. You will retype it in single line spacing and it will only take up one page.

2 Read the assignment through before you begin and consider appropriate display.

3 Type carefully, inserting all the manuscript portions correctly and considering the context of what you are typing. Make sure it makes sense.

Pointers

SEMINAR ROOMS

~~There are~~ 12 seminar rooms, each 31 sq m~~etres~~ ~~(337 sq feet)~~. Can accommodate 10 persons, These rooms ~~located on the third level~~ are ~~/perfect for~~ particularly suitable for small meetings and workshop sessions.

boardroom style.

← Spell 'accommodate' correctly, as shown here.

← Insert the information from the balloons in the correct places.

EQUIPMENT AND SUPPORT SERVICES

~~Audio-Visual Equipment~~

VHS video recorder ~~with PAL, NTSC, SECAM systems~~ and

Compact disc equipment

Table, free-standing and ~~wireless~~ cordless microphones

close up — P A system with fixed and portable loudspeakers

Slide, overhead and 16 mm movie projectors with rear projection facilities

~~Simultaneous interpretation control unit~~

~~Portable laser karaoke system~~

Electronic pointer

~~Facsimile~~ FAX and photocopier available in adjacent Business Centre

Telephone,

~~Conference Presentation~~

Podiums and lecterns

Notice Boards and

Easels

~~Portable platforms/stages~~

Wall, partitions and overhead track system provide good acoustic performance with minimum sound loss. Facilities include motorised screen, curtain remote control, automatic airconditioning.

← List these items in single spacing.

3 You are secretary to Mrs Rachel Thaxton, Secretarial Services Manager of Comlon International plc. Stephen Bowler is Head of Administration.
(SSC – 2 December 1992)

Pointers

Memo to Stephen Bowler

OFFICE TECHNOLOGY 2000

I attach some literature which I brought back from the Office Technology conference which I attended last week.

← These first two paragraphs are straightforward.

NP [I was particularly interested in the talk about EDI, which I think the Company should consider.

← Remember a capital 'C' for 'Company' as this refers to Comlon.

Please continue with the following amended typescript describing EDI and add final para. as shown.

← The balloon contains an instruction for you.

Pointers

(Add to memo to Mr Bowler)

NP [EDI (Electronic Document Interchange) is a /further move towards the paperless

office. All the details of a transaction are handled electronically from the

packing slip, to the customs forms to *and* the invoice to the final transfer of

funds; electrically with the minimum use of paper. The importance *The* /*of such a system* will become

apparent with the full implementation of the European Common Market.

NP [The shipping industry is already adopting /*EDI. This* the system which would be

particularly advantageous to a company such as ours with our overseas

connections. *and the need to move large quantities of*
raw materials and finished goods.

NP [EDI is much more than just a question of using an electronic medium to transfer

information. EDI To be effective /*EDI requires* is a total business approach. It is about *and*

fundamental changes to the way business is carried out; It cannot just be

appended to existing business methods.

NP [Dealing with the security and auditing problems of EDI requires a structured *is complicated.*

and formal approach. Guarding EDI against fraud and manipulation means

developing sophisticated mechanisms for authenticating orders. This involves

key generation, digital signatures derived from encryption processes, not *similar*

unlike *To* the use of personal identification numbers but more complex, and the use

of non-repudiation techniques.

NP If the Company considers /*using* any of the courses on *sincerely, that*
EDI mentioned in the literature I /hope /some
of the senior secretaries may be involved.

← Can you understand all the printers' correction signs shown in the left margin?

← Insert handwritten details correctly.

Notes

1 This assignment also extends to two pages. Use appropriate paper and include all essential details at the top.

2 Transcribe carefully from the amended typescript. Make sure you do not lose your place or it would be easy to omit a whole line or part of a line.

3 Read everything as you transcribe, to ensure that everything is making proper sense.

4 The first paragraph of the memo says 'I attach . . .' so why not write 'Enc' at the bottom of the second page so that you do not forget it at the end of the memo?

4 You are secretary to Mrs Anne Richards, Conferences Manager (Administration), Comlon International plc. Brian Summers is Training Officer, Business Techniques plc, 74 Shenton Road, London W10 9AP. *(SSC – 9 June 1993)*

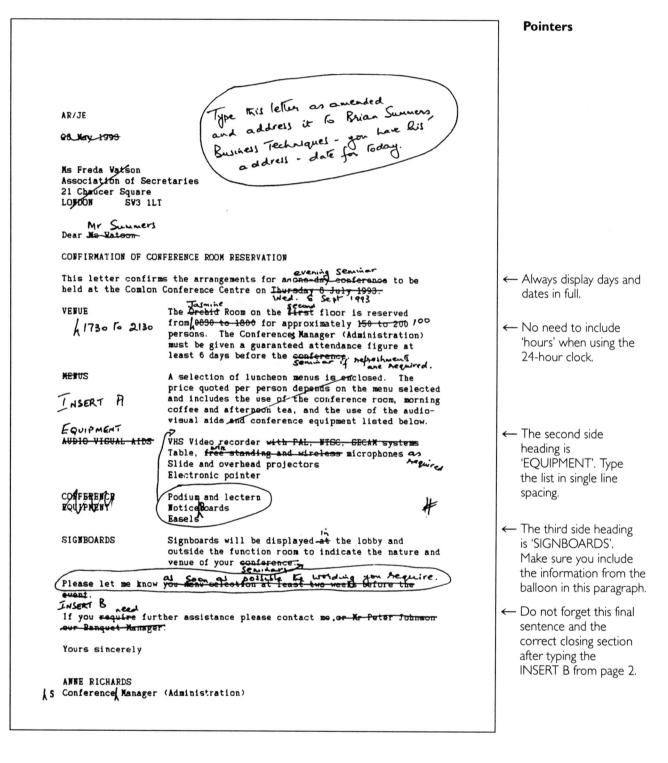

Pointers

← Always display days and dates in full.

← No need to include 'hours' when using the 24-hour clock.

← The second side heading is 'EQUIPMENT'. Type the list in single line spacing.

← The third side heading is 'SIGNBOARDS'. Make sure you include the information from the balloon in this paragraph.

← Do not forget this final sentence and the correct closing section after typing the INSERT B from page 2.

Notes

1 This assignment again extends to two pages. Study the requirements carefully. You will see that you will be typing quite a long letter which will extend to two pages. Remember this when approaching the bottom of page one, so that you have sufficient details to take to a second page.

2 Do you need to refer back to Specimen Document Layouts to check the correct way to head a continuation sheet?

3 Your employer has noted 'INSERT A' and 'INSERT B' on the letter. These should not be typed; they are instructions for you to insert the information which is drafted on the second page.

4 Consider the context of what you are typing. Make sure it makes sense.

Letter to Mr Summers - carry on under VENUE

INSERT A — The seminar room booking includes the use of the equipment listed below. Tea/coffee and light refreshments can be supplied for an additional charge as shown on the enclosed price list.

INSERT B

TERMS — Payment of the total cost incurred, including food and beverages, must be made upon presentation of the bill.

CANCELLATION CHARGE — In the event of cancellation of your function after 1 Sept '93 a cancellation charge of 30% of the total estimated bill will be levied.

← These manuscript notes must be inserted at the appropriate point as instructed on the original letter.

5 You are secretary to Mrs Jane Harris, Advertising and Marketing Support, Comlon International plc. This letter should be addressed to Mr Frederick S Wyatt, Advertising and Promotions, Comlon International plc, Comlon House, 1222 Park Avenue, NY 10005, New York, USA. (Assignment 2 mentioned on page two of this assignment can be found on page 66). (PSC – 16 June 1993)

Pointers

> *Adapt this letter and address it to Mr Wyatt in New York. Change the names and places as appropriate and include the insertions on the next page. The American Conference was at the Regency Hotel, New York.*

```
Mr John W Ferguson
Director, Publicity
Comlon International plc
Comlon House
Monmouth Street
Toronto
Ontario    M6P 2M5
CANADA
```

Dear ~~John~~ *Frederick*   ← 1

Thank you very much indeed for your hospitality while I was in Toronto and for sparing so much of your time to show me round your organisation.   ← 2

I appreciated the meetings and discussions I had with members of your Publicity Department and I am very grateful for the help and advice I was given. The Conference at the Sheraton Towers was particularly interesting and gave me the opportunity to meet representatives and franchise holders from many parts of Canada. I understand how important it is to take account of regional differences when mounting a major advertising campaign. *(Insert 1)*   ← 3 ← 4 ← 5

Since my return I have had several ideas about the advertising and promotion of the new franchises shortly to be operational ~~in this country~~ *here* and I shall be discussing my ideas soon with Paul King.

[As you know it has been decided that fish will be the speciality food offered in the new outlets.] *Insert 2*   ← 6

Stet [I shall look forward to having further discussions with you when you next visit this country.]   ← 7

Yours sincerely


```
JANE HARRIS
Advertising and Marketing Support
```

Key

1 Note the personalised salutation 'Dear Frederick'.

2 Mr Wyatt is not in Toronto. You will type 'New York'.

3 What is the name of Mr Wyatt's department?

4 Where was the American Conference held?

5 Instead of 'Canada', what will you type?

6 This paragraph has to be deleted and you must insert other details in its place.

7 'Stet' means this paragraph must not be deleted as originally instructed. This will be the final paragraph of the letter after typing 'Insert 2' from the second page.

Pointers

Insert 1   I was surprised to learn that children under 12 years of age provide such a large part of the business of the American franchises and I am giving special consideration to the viability of a similar potential market here. *in this country*

INSERT 2   Most of the methods I have suggested have already been tried successfully in the United States & Canada but there are two ideas about which I should like to have your opinion regarding promotions to appeal to young people. These suggestions are

> Typist: Please insert nos 2.4 & 2.5 from Assignment 2, re-numbered as 1 and 2

← Refer back to page 66 and type the numbered points correctly.

NP   [I should be interested to hear whether you have used similar devices to advertise speciality foods in these outlets *in America*. If so I should be grateful for any information or advice you can give me.

stet

← After this paragraph remember to refer back to the original letter for the closing paragraph.

Notes

1 Here is another two page assignment, so again this letter will extend to a continuation sheet. Remember this as you type the first page to avoid cramming the entire letter on one page.

2 Here, a letter has already been sent to Mr John W Ferguson in Toronto. Your employer has adapted a copy of this letter so that a new letter can be sent to Mr Wyatt in New York.

3 Again the second page of the assignment contains 'Insert 1' and 'Insert 2'. Check the original letter carefully so that you insert the correct paragraphs at the appropriate points.

4 The employer refers to information which must be copied from another document already produced. You will find relevant details at the head of this assignment.

6 You are secretary to Mrs Margaret Johnson, Customer Relations Manager, Comlon International plc. *(PSC – Specimen, 15 June 1992)*

Pointers

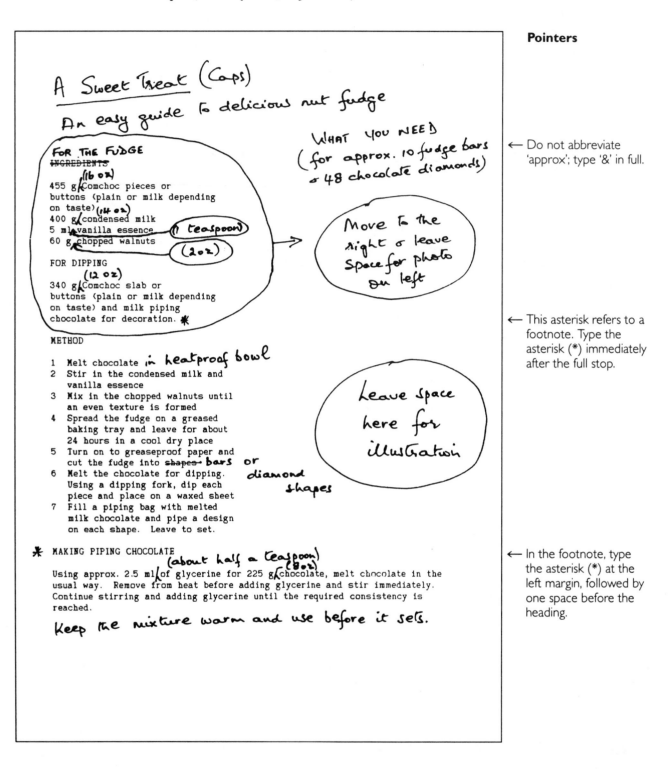

← Do not abbreviate 'approx'; type '&' in full.

← This asterisk refers to a footnote. Type the asterisk (*) immediately after the full stop.

← In the footnote, type the asterisk (*) at the left margin, followed by one space before the heading.

Notes

1 This is different – a recipe. It must be displayed attractively, on one page only.

2 After the main headings, follow the instructions to leave a space on the left for a photo opposite the ingredients. To balance out the recipe, there will be a space on the right for an illustration opposite the method.

3 In the list of ingredients, correct spacing is shown and abbreviations are acceptable, eg 455 g, 16 oz, 5 ml. Copy the ingredients carefully.

4 Remember to include reference and date at the bottom left.

3.4 Special assignments

Apart from general business correspondence like letters and memos and straightforward revision of material, you will be required to transcribe other business documents. In Unit 2 we looked at a variety of documents which may be included in the examination. Many of these documents will be studied in other components of your examination, ie Communication – Use of English and Office Organisation and Secretarial Procedures, eg itineraries, meetings documents, etc.

In the Manuscript Transcription examination you will be required to interpret your employer's instructions and ensure that information is displayed appropriately. There will probably be links with other assignments from which extracts may have to be taken, and information may have to be rearranged. You will be required to consider the purpose of the document. It will be up to you to ensure that documents are presented in a suitable format.

EXAMPLE 1 (worked)

You are secretary to Mrs Rachel Thaxton, Secretarial Services Manager, Comlon International plc. *(SSC – 2 December 1992)*

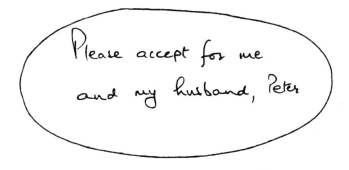

```
                    COMLON INTERNATIONAL (TURIN) plc

        The Chairman and Directors request the pleasure of the company of

    _____MRS___RACHEL_THAXTON_AND__PARTNER_____

            at the opening of the EXHIBITION OF LA SETA DI TORINO

                        at the Silkweavers Hall

                            Silk Street

                    London        EC4 9HY

                    on Thursday 21 January 1993

    RSVP                                          1900 for 1930
    Mrs J Davidson                            Buffet Supper 2000
    Public Relations Officer
    Room 603                              Exhibition closes 2200
    Comlon House
    SW1Y 2AR
```

Please accept for me and my husband, Peter

Mrs Thaxton has received an invitation and has written instructions for you to compose a reply.

Examination approach

- Read the incoming invitation carefully, noting that it is written formally and in third person.

- Note who has issued the invitation and the name of the company.

- Note all the specific details – the function, the date, the venue.

- Check the name to whom replies should be forwarded (RSVP).

- Plan a reply incorporating all the essential details and using the same style as the original, ie third person.

Examiner's check copy

In this case, two different approaches are illustrated. Both of them would
be acceptable.

Comlon International plc

Comlon House West Street London SW1Y 2AR

tel: 0181 302 0261
telex: Comlond 888941   telemessages: Comlond London SW1   fax: 0181 302 4169

RT/ST

2 December 1992

Mrs J Davidson
Public Relations Officer
Comlon International (Turin) plc
Room 603
Comlon House
London
SW1Y 2AR

Mrs Rachel Thaxton thanks the Chairman and Directors of
Comlon International (Turin) plc for their kind invitation to
the opening of the Exhibition of La Seta di Torino to be held
at the Silkweavers Hall, London on Thursday 21 January 1993.

Mrs Thaxton has much pleasure in accepting for herself and
her husband, Mr Peter Thaxton.

← Letterheaded paper.

← Opening details as in a
business letter.

← A straightforward paragraph
written in third person
acknowledging the invitation.
Include details of the function
and the date.
← An appropriately-worded
acceptance.

Mrs Rachel Thaxton
and Mr Peter Thaxton

thank the Chairman and Directors of
Comlon International (Turin) plc

for their kind invitation to the
opening of the

EXHIBITION OF LA SETA DI TORINO

at the Silkweavers Hall
Silk Street, London

on Thursday 21 January 1993

and have much pleasure in accepting

Comlon International plc
Comlon House
West Street   RT/ST
London SW1Y 2AR   2 December 1992

← In this example, the
reply has been typed in
a similar format to the
original invitation. Third
person is used.

← Mention function and date.

← Include acceptance.

← The sender's address is
noted at the foot
together with
reference/date.

Marked answer

Comlon International plc

Comlon House West Street London SW1Y 2AR

tel: 0181 302 0261
telex: Comlond 888941   telemessages: Comlond London SW1   fax: 0181 302 4169

M E M O R A N D U M   *Memo*   -1

To   Mrs J Davidson, Public Relations Officer
From   Mrs Rachel Thaxton   (*title ?*)   -1
Ref   RT/PG
Date   2 December 1992

ACCEPT INVITATION   -1
                    the   *opening* ....   -1 -1
I have received invitation to the Exhibition of La Seta Di
Torino and accept the invitation for myself and husband,
Peter.

Thank you.   *day/date*   -1

                                              third person   -1

                    Total Penalties = 7

Display

1 Although letterheaded paper has been correctly used, the candidate has used the memo format, which is incorrect.

2 The display of the TO/FROM/REF/DATE section is unattractive, although this has not been penalised. It would have looked better with all the information against the headings starting at the same point.

3 A title has been shown for Mrs Davidson but not for Mrs Thaxton. Consistency is expected.

4 A more suitable heading should have been composed.

Transcription

1 Third person should be used when responding to invitations.

2 Definite and indefinite articles are often omitted. In this case, 'the' before 'invitation'.

3 The candidate has not included the fact that the invitation is to 'the opening' of this exhibition. The date has also been omitted.

4 Instead of 'Thank you' a more appropriate expression should have been used.

EXAMPLE 2 (analysis)

You are secretary to Mrs Anne Richards, Conferences Manager (Administration), Comlon International plc. The company's organisation chart shows the following information: Mark McNally, Conferences Manager (Display and Exhibits); Sarah Fletcher, Deputy Conference Manager; Jill Cartwright, Support Systems Organiser; Dominic Mason, Programme Organiser. *(SSC – 9 June 1993)*

Pointers

Send a memo to Mark McNally with copies to Dominic Mason, Jill Cartwright & Sarah Fletcher. Tell them that the next monthly Planning Meeting will be held in my office at 1000 on Monday next (add the date). As the main item for discussion will be the conference & exhibition to be held in Birmingham next May will they please come prepared to report on progress to date in their areas. Include the following Agenda –

1   Minutes of last meeting
2   Matters arising
3   Arrangements for Birmingham Conference
     10 – 13 May 1994
3.1   Administration (Anne Richards to report)
3.2   Display & Exhibits (M McNally & S Fletcher)
3.3   Programme (Dominic Mason)
3.4   Support Systems (J Cartwright).
4   New Edinburgh Conference Centre
     (A Richards to report development progress)

5   A O B
6   Date & time of next meeting
     (Same time, 3rd Monday in July)

for manufacturers and distributors of self-assembly furniture

© LCCI 1993

← Although the instructions state that this is to be typed as a memo, it's up to you to decide on a suitable layout within the body of the memo, ie displaying the agenda appropriately.

← Remember the verbs 'send', 'tell them', 'add', 'Include' etc are specific instructions to you, stating what you should include in the memo.

Marked answer

Here is one candidate's answer, with notes from the examiner.

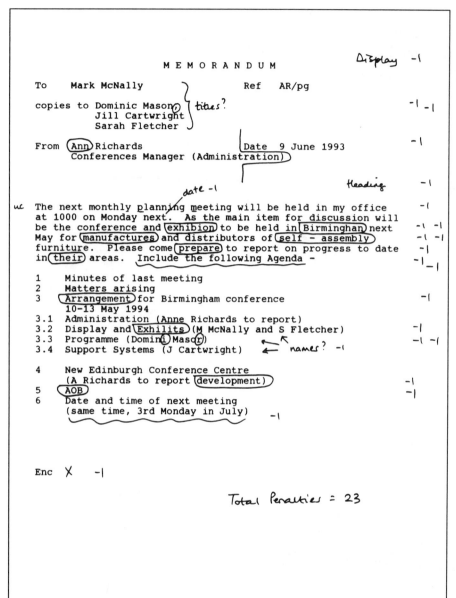

Display

1 The overall appearance of this memo is not pleasing to the eye. Mrs Richards' title runs along under the date, and it would have been better to show the list of people receiving copies at the foot of the memo.

2 Designations should have been shown for all recipients, and those receiving copies should have been listed in alphabetical order.

3 A heading should have been composed.

4 No attempt has been made to display the agenda appropriately. The employer's outline has simply been copied, instead of displaying the information to the best advantage.

5 'Enc' is unnecessary.

Transcription

1 The employer's first name 'Anne' has been misspelled.

2 Initial capitals for 'Planning Meeting' were clearly indicated in the manuscript.

3 A date should have been provided for the next meeting.

4 The second sentence is incomplete.

5 'self-assembly' is a hyphenated compound word so there should be no space either side of the hyphen.

6 The candidate has not changed the pronoun 'their' to 'your'.

7 'Include the following Agenda' should have been read as an instruction to the candidate, not to be typed.

A simple heading 'AGENDA' at the left margin was required.

8 The candidate has copied names as written instead of ensuring consistency by including all first names.

9 'AOB' (Any Other Business) should have been transcribed in full.

10 The appropriate time and date should have been included.

11 There are several careless spelling and typographical errors, although the words are correctly spelled in the manuscript copy (exhibition, Birmingham, Arrangements, Exhibits, Dominic Mason, developments).

Can you do better?

Transcribe this assignment yourself and then compare your work with the check copy on page 179.

TRANSCRIPTION TIPS FOR PRACTICAL ASSIGNMENTS

Special assignments

1 Locate any specific instructions which tell you what to do.

2 Read through the assignment carefully, considering the purpose of the document.

3 Check correction signs, amendments and insertions so that you interpret them correctly.

4 Make any necessary calculations.

5 Consider specific presentation requirements, and make a rough draft if necessary, eg for a notice/advertisement/invitation/ agenda/minutes.

6 Remember to include reference and date.

7 Choose appropriate paper and transcribe the assignment carefully.

8 Check for errors.

PRACTICAL ASSIGNMENTS

1 You are secretary to Mrs Rachel Thaxton, Secretarial Services Manager, Comlon International. The following information was shown on the organisation chart on the examination paper: Brian Haywood, Training Officer
Joanne E Laws, Personnel Officer *(SSC – 2 December 1992)*

Pointers

ONE-DAY INDUCTION COURSE FOR NEW SECRETARIAL STAFF

MONDAY 1 Feb 1993

in the Comlon House Theatre

0900 Introduction Stephen Curtis
Training Supervisor

0930 Secretarial services and Company
Career structure   R_T... Sec. Services Man.

1015 Coffee

1030 Video "Silks and Satins"
A view of the work of the Company presented
by B... H..- Training Officer

1130 Personnel Dept
Aug J..- E Laws

1215 Lunch

1330 Assemble in Theatre

Groups to tour the following admin. departments

PRINT AND REPROGRAPHIC
CENTRAL COMPUTER   (please arrange
TRAVEL   alphabetically)
MAIL
TELEPHONE EXCHANGE

1600 Tea

Disperse to departments

← Type the date in full.

← Retain capitals as on the original, but remember to arrange alphabetically.

Notes

1 This is a simple programme for the Company's induction course. Use plain paper.

2 Consider how you will display the programme, with timing at the left margin and each item blocked alongside.

3 Be consistent in display of each item. Why not type the programme items on one line with name and title of presenter beneath it?

4 Present full names and titles consistently.

5 Remember the reference and date at the bottom left.

2 You are secretary to Mark Davidson, Manager, Advertising and Marketing Department, Comlon International plc. *(SSC – 8 June 1994)*

(Please display attractively)

CREATIVE TOYS

Powered by Imagination!

Your child's imagination is as big as it is allowed to be.
Creative toys stimulate imagination and creativity

½ Comlon toys presents 4 new creative and imaginative lines:

1 Create Your Own
2 Build Your Own
3 Make Your Own
4 Power Your Own

Ready for Christmas 1994!

For free illustrated catalogue write to (my name, address etc)
or telephone FREEPHONE COMLON

← Consider how you will display this advertisement to best advantage. Remember that there is no 'correct' display – just use some creative flair and make sure it looks eye-catching.

← Include your employer's full name, title, company and address.

Notes

I This is an advertisement so any appropriate display would be acceptable.

2 Try to centre the advertisement both vertically and horizontally, to make full use of the paper.

3 Remember a reference and date must be included.

3 You are secretary to Mrs Jane Harris, Advertising and Marketing Support, Comlon International plc. *(PSC – 16 June 1993)*

Pointers

Please type a notice for staff noticeboards – display effectively

Secretary/Administrator required for Advertising & Marketing Support to assist with the advertising & promotion of fast food outlets. This is a Grade 5 post to be filled by an employee ~~hardly scored~~ and with a minimum of 3 years' service in the Company with experience at senior secretary level.

← Why not centre the job title and opening details?

The successful applicant will be ~~working for~~ ~~responsible to~~ *stet* Mrs Jane Harris but must be prepared to work independently and/to use initiative & imagination in helping to launch new outlets. Ability to use ~~existing~~ the Company computer system and WP software is essential; secretarial/administrative qualifications also essential. ~~advantageous~~. Specialised training in advertising and marketing techniques will be given to an/enthusiastic suitably qualified applicant. Application forms may be obtained from Departmental Managers and must be returned by 5 July to Personnel Department Room 205 Comlon House

← Remember to paragraph appropriately.

← Why not centre the final details attractively?

Notes

1 Here is another assignment requiring creative flair. This time it is an internal notice.

2 Study the content carefully and note where new lines will begin, and where you will begin new paragraphs.

3 There is no need to centre every line of the notice. The main text can be blocked.

4 Once again, remember to include reference and date.

4 You are secretary to Geoff Brady, Manager (Coaches), Comlon International plc.
   (PSC – 8 December 1993)

Comlon International plc, Comlon House etc

Booking Form for UK Coach Excursions 1994

Destination   Excursion No   Departure Date
_____

Name (Mr/Mrs/Miss/Ms)

_____

Address

_____

_____

_____

Post Code _____   Telephone No. _____

Names of others included in this Booking
(Please give initials)

_____

_____

_____

Coach Boarding Point _____

I enclose cheque for _____ OR

Please debit my _____ Account to the amount of £ ____

Card no. _____ Expiry date _____

Address (if different from above) _____

_____

_____

Signature _____   Date _____

Pointers

← Company details are included as a heading – this is not an instruction to use letterheaded paper.

← Leave sufficient space beneath these first headings so that details can be inserted. (Clue: More space may be needed for 'Destination' than 'Excursion No' or 'Departure Date'.)

← Remember to use double line spacing.

Notes

1 This time you have to design a form. Follow the general layout indicated in your employer's rough draft.

2 Use continuous dots or underscore for the lines where information will be completed. Leave one space before each line starts.

3 Enhance display by using equal left and right margins.

4 Consider details which will be inserted and leave appropriate space.

5 You are secretary to Mrs Barbara Ashton, Marketing Development Manager, Comlon International plc. *(PSC – 15 June 1994)* You have been asked to type out a recipe to send to MR KEITH DAVIS, MANAGER, CHEESE, DAIRY, FROZEN FOOD DEPARTMENT as a contribution to the CHRISTMAS 1994 SPECIAL PROMOTION – BLUE CHEESE DAY. (NB: Use similar headings to the assignment shown on page 69. *(PSC – 15 June 1994)*

BLUE CHEESE PASTA

Ingredients
350 g tagliatelle
1 small onion
1 red pepper   } Sliced
1 courgette
225 g gammon

1 tbs walnut oil

100 g chestnut mushrooms
10 g flour
10 g butter
300 ml milk
50 g blue cheese

Method
1. Cook tagliatelle according to instructions on the packet. 2 Fry onion in oil until soft. 3 Add gammon, pepper, stir in courgette and mushrooms. 4 cook on low heat for 5 minutes. 5 heat butter in separate pan over low heat; add flour and stir to smooth paste. 6 gradually add milk and cook until thickened, stirring all the time. 7 Stir in crumbled blue cheese.

To serve Place pasta on warm plates, spoon gammon mixture in centre and drizzle with sauce.

Pointers

← Abbreviations can be retained in the list of ingredients, ie 350 g, 1 tbs, 50 g.

← Do not bracket the walnut oil with the other items – it would be very difficult to slice!

← Display the numbered points on separate lines, with double line spacing between each point.

Notes

1 Read the instructions at the head of this assignment carefully. You are given advice about the display of headings for this recipe.

2 The first 5 ingredients need bracketing together. Type 5 right-hand brackets beneath one another, with the word 'sliced' alongside.

3 Read the 'Method' section through carefully before transcribing, so that you are familiar with the content.

4 Transcribe carefully so that no wording is omitted, and take extra care with spellings.

5 Remember to include reference and date.

6 You are secretary to Mrs Jane Harris, Advertising and Marketing Support, Comlon
International plc. *(PSC – 16 June 1993)*

EXPENSES – MAY 1993

*Please type & fill
in the amounts
for me*

Visit to Brighton new
franchise & transport of
publicity material –
165 miles at 30p per mile   – – – – –   ← Type the amounts in a
column at the right-
hand side where
Advance publicity by courier £30   – – – – –   indicated by the dots.

Visit to Colchester to discuss new
franchise publicity in South-east
England & East Anglia
(first class)
Return / rail fare £35.50
Taxis   20.00   – – – –   ← Add the two figures
together and type
the total in the right-
hand column.

Additional expenses from visit to
USA & Canada to study
franchise publicity.
Taxi: London Heathrow to home £50   – – – –

                                Total   – – –   ← Insert underscore
above and below the
total amount.

Retained American dollars $200 less
$50 for airport tax & taxi between
New York hotel & John F Kennedy Airport =
    $150 converted to sterling at
    $1.50 = £1 = £ – – – –

Amount to be claimed   – – – –   ← The amount to be
claimed will be the total
of the main
items minus the
amount retained.

Notes

1 This is an account of expenses incurred by your employer
on a recent trip.

2 Use a calculator and make notes before transcribing.
Study the items carefully and make calculations correctly,
especially the currency conversions at the bottom.

3 Do not forget reference and date.

7 You are secretary to Miss Jane Wittington, Editor of Sweet News, Comlon
International plc. *(PSC – 9 December 1992)*

Pointers

NOTICE

The monthly meeting of the Sweet News Magazine Committee will be held at
1400 on Monday 7 December 1992 in Room 216 Comlon House.

JANE WITTINGTON (Miss)
Editor

AGENDA   CHAIRMAN'S NOTES

                                                   Ms Flood

1 Apologies for absence   –

2 Minutes of meeting held on 2 November 1992 – circulated, approved & signed

3 Matters arising from the Minutes – Press Officer reported clearance in time for Dec. issue

   3.1 Copyright clearance on Article 4

4 Late contributions for December issue – None

5 Coverage of annual staff prize awards 1993 – Editor arranging conference facilities, Westin Slough – To report at next meeting

6 Special edition for Centenary, July 1993 → Subcommittee appointed – Chairman M Gardner Members S Hardwick & J Stanford – to report at next meeting

7 Any other business – None

8 Date and time of next meeting
   11 Jan '93 usual time & place

Copies to: Jane Wittington, Editor and Chairman
            Jessica Flood, Human Resources Manager
            Martin Gardner, Press Officer
            Sophie Hardwick, Secretarial and Clerical Representative
            Peter Laker, Production Representative
            David Masters, Purchasing Representative
            James Stanford, Administration

Please prepare Minutes for meeting held on 7 Dec.
Also Notice & Agenda for next meeting – usual
items plus reports on items 5 & 6 arising from
Minutes. Late contributions for Jan. issue will
have to be held until Feb. unless very topical as
publication date is 25 Jan. Before A.O.B. please
include new format of Sweet News for discussion.
(No need to type full list of names at the end
of Minutes – just Copies to All Committee Members)
                                                    JW

← Use full sentences
  to expand hand-
  written notes.

← Type all names in full.

← Read carefully and
  understand the
  instructions in
  this balloon
  before attempting
  this assignment.

← Draft out the
  Notice/Agenda before
  typing, following the
  instructions in this
  section. Use the same
  display as in the original
  shown here.

Notes

1 Your employer has written notes on her copy of this
meeting Agenda. She instructs you to prepare two
documents – Minutes of this meeting and a
Notice/Agenda for the next meeting.

2 Refer to the Specimen Document Formats for guidelines
on display of these documents.

3 Transcribe the Minutes first, expanding the employer's
notes appropriately and using third person and reported
speech. Remember that full sentences must be used, eg
for item 3.1: 'Mr . . ., Press Officer, reported that copyright
clearance on Article 4 had been received in time for the
December issue.'

4 Remember that the Minutes must be able to be read and
understood by members who were absent from the
meeting. Make sure what you are typing makes sense.

8 You are secretary to Mrs Barbara Ashton, Marketing Development Manager, Comlon International plc. Mrs Ashton leaves on 6 September on a business trip to South East Asia. *(PSC – 15 June 1994)*

Pointers

> Overseas trip I have jotted down the details I have so far. Please type a draft itinerary for me. It's beginning to take shape!

Depart LHR BA 011 2145 Tues. 6 Sept.
Arr Singapore Changi 1750 Wed. 7 "
Dep Singapore 0915 Mon 12/9 MAS 15
Arr Kuala Lumpur Subang 1000 12/9
Dep. K.L. 0800 Wed 14/9 MAS 26
Arr Kuching International 0930
Dep Kuching 16/9 0700 (Shuttle)
Arr Singapore 0830 Dep 1015 SA 125
Arr Hong Kong Kai Tak 1345
Dep Hong Kong Tues 20/9 2100 BA 021
Arr LHR 21/9 1330 Car to home

Hotels   Singapore - Mandarin, Orchard Road
K.L. Ming Court [Kuching, Holiday Inn;
Hong Kong, Royal Pacific

Confirmed appointments to date: / Singapore - Thurs 8/9 1000
Mr Charles Wang, Fortune Foods; Fri 9/9 1130
visit to Far East Trading. Mon. 12/9 (KL)
Contact Mr Ken Taylor on arrival. Wed 14/9 -
Contact Mr Peter Ho (Kuching); Fri 16/9 meet
Mr Chen Li at airport (HK)

← 'LHR' means 'London Heathrow Airport'.

← Type 'Depart' and 'Arrive' in full.

← Type the abbreviation 'K.L.' in full.

← Your finished itinerary will not have these headings 'Hotels' and 'Confirmed appointments to date'. You must incorporate these details under the relevant dates on the itinerary.

Notes

1 Your employer wants you to draft an itinerary for her forthcoming trip. Refer back to the Specimen Document Formats and consider an appropriate display.

2 As this is a draft, remember to type 'DRAFT' at the top left.

3 Compose suitable headings (whose trip? where? when?).

4 The first subheading will be TUESDAY 6 SEPTEMBER. Write down everything happening on that date, using two columns as shown in the specimen. Use days/dates as subheadings throughout the itinerary.

5 Remember to expand all abbreviations and dates.

6 Write out the itinerary in rough first, so that you remember all relevant details under each date.

Part D

Manuscript transcription: the examination

If you have worked through Unit 3 you should by now be very familiar with the unique requirements of the Manuscript Transcription examination. You have had to think carefully and use your initiative to interpret written instructions. You have had to decide on an appropriate format for each document and ensure that the employer's meaning is accurately expressed. You will appreciate that this is a very realistic examination which tests your transcription ability in a practical office situation.

It is hoped that in working through the assignments in Unit 3 you have built up your confidence in transcribing from written instructions given in different ways. You should now be ready to tackle complete examination papers.

In the examination, as in the office, common vocabulary and language will be used. There will probably be a common theme connecting some of the assignments. This will make it easier for you to think yourself into the position of secretary as described on the Instruction Sheet.

In an office you would not transcribe anything for your employer unless you have studied it carefully and understood completely what was required. In the examination too, it is imperative that you spend time reading, interpreting and trying to understand the requirements. In this section you will learn how to do this, how to put everything together, how to help yourself so that you can approach the examination confidently.

Unit 4

Examination technique

By the end of this unit you will be able to:

- *appreciate the aims, expectations and content of the Manuscript Transcription examination*

- *identify the main reasons why marks may be deducted*

- *recognise the steps which should be taken to be successful in the examination*

Aims and expectations

The main aim of the examination is '. . . to produce business documents from written instructions in a form which would be acceptable for signature by an employer.'

The examination will include six assignments, and with the requirement for an approximate production speed of 45 wpm, this should be well within most candidates' capabilities. However, it is still possible to pass the examination without completing all the assignments, provided the work produced has been completed accurately and appropriately.

Examination timing

Before the transcription time commences, you will be allowed 15 minutes to read through the examination paper. This time should be used wisely. So much time in the examination is often wasted by starting and scrapping assignments because of failing to understand the requirements before transcribing. This can be avoided by careful reading and thoughtful preparation of work during the 15 minutes' reading time.

With proper preparation, there should be ample time to transcribe the six tasks in the two hours' transcription time allowed.

Main reasons for penalties

After every examination, the Chief Examiner writes a report giving an overall opinion on candidates' work together with helpful comments. From a study of these reports over the last few years, it can be seen that candidates make the same errors year after year. Most of the typical errors have been included in the marked answers in Unit 3. Here we look at a summary of all the main areas of concern:

Poor spelling

Many spelling errors are made in words which appear on the Instruction Sheet or on the examination paper. Such errors may be due to rushing work, but this should not be necessary if work has been prepared thoughtfully and checked carefully. Variations in spellings are acceptable, eg color/colour, provided they are used consistently, but more care should be taken in checking work. If a word processor is used, it is advisable to use a spell check in the examination, but remember that a spell check will not highlight mistypes such as 'charge' instead of 'change'.

Typographical errors

Again, many careless typographical errors are made. This shows that time is not being used widely for preparation, checking and proofreading. Secretaries must be able to check their own work before presentation to their employers. Careless work would not be acceptable.

Mistranscription

The 15 minutes' reading time before commencing transcription should be used wisely. There is common vocabulary throughout several assignments, so it is frustrating for examiners when words are transcribed correctly in one assignment but incorrectly in another. In some cases, sentences do not make any sense. So many of these errors could be avoided through better reading, preparation and thoughtful transcription. Variations in transcription are acceptable as long as the message is clear and the employer's meaning has been accurately expressed.

Poor grammar

Grammatical errors are frequently made in subject/verb agreement, mixing tenses and incorrect use of pronouns. If necessary, extra practice must be given to help students with particular problems in these areas.

Poor composition

Considerable practice is needed in the art of composing brief, clear and grammatically correct communications. In particular, you must learn to:

● distinguish between notes from the employer to the secretary and information to be included in the actual communication.

● consider who is receiving the message, and use an appropriate tone.

● think like the person sending the message. In this way, confusion between pronouns such as 'you' and 'her', 'his' and 'your' etc, should be avoided.

● remember that material sometimes needs to be rearranged to ensure a logical structure.

Poor proofreading

Each assignment should be checked carefully before moving on to the next. It defeats the objective if all six assignments are transcribed but they are too inaccurate to be signed. It is possible to pass the examination with 5 completed assignments if these are accurate enough and well displayed.

Poor presentation

In this examination you are not required simply to copy from manuscript. Initiative is required to ensure that documents contain all relevant details and are displayed in an appropriate format.

It is particularly disappointing to have to deduct marks for errors in layout and display. However, the following presentation errors constantly recur:

Letters
Omission of courtesy title for addressees

```
John Smith
Managing Director
Futura Chemicals Inc
24 Long Lane
42000 KUALA LUMPUR
West Malaysia
```

Incorrect salutation or complimentary close

```
Dear John
```

```
Yours sincerely
```

Incorrect display of name or title

```
        Mrs Sheila Byrde (Administrative Manager)
```

Memos

Inconsistent details provided about sender or recipient

```
M E M O R A N D U M

To    Mrs Kim Marshall, Secretarial Services Manager

From  Judy Wong

Ref   JW/PG

Date  2 June 19--
```

Omission of subject heading

```
M E M O R A N D U M

To    Patricia Farrelly, Sales and Marketing Director

From  Rosehannah McLellan, Sales Manager

Ref   RM/PG

Date  2 June 19--



All the arrangements for my trip are now finalised and I
leave next Wednesday.
```

General

Cramming a two-page document onto one page

```
      Whether you are visiting friends or relatives, or taking the
      holiday of a life time, I will be delighted to offer the
      assurance and advice you need.

      I hope to hear from you soon.

      Yours faithfully

      EDITH EMERSON (Manageress)    Enc
```

Using letterheaded paper instead of plain for continuation sheets or
for memos

Comlon International plc

Comlon House West Street London SW1Y 2AR

tel: 0181 302 0261
telex: Comlond 888941   telemessages: Comlond London SW1   fax: 0181 302 4169

2
DG/PG
2 June 19--
Mrs Della Newley

Unsuitable display for special assignments

```
      - - - - - - - - - - - - - - - - - - - - - - - - - - - - - - - -

      Please return to me by end of next month.


      Cheque enclosed for £.. in payment of deposit.
      Name .................. Address ..............................
```

Omission of continuation sheet headings and carrying insufficient details to second page

```
Page 2



Best wishes

Yours sincerely



DANIEL BOLAN
Public Relations Manager
```

Retention of abbreviations such as 'he'd', 'I'll', 'phone', etc

```
     I've been talking to my Manager and he'd like to discuss this
     with you if you'll attend a meeting next Monday.
```

Inconsistent layout and spacing (in this example the heading is blocked so data beneath column headings should also be blocked; also unequal spacing between columns)

```
     CANADIAN WEATHER
     Average Temperatures

                    Spring      Summer   Autumn   Winter
     Western Canada    56          74       58       48
     Central Canada    46          77       52       37
     Eastern Canada    48          73       57       48
```

Inconsistent display of numbers, dates, times, names, etc

```
     Thank you for your letter dated 5 June.  I have noted your
     reservation of two single rooms and 4 doubles for August 8th.
```

Omission of enclosures or routing

> I have passed your comments on to Mark Campbell in Public Relations and he will make appropriate investigations.
>
> In the meantime, our cheque for £4.85 is enclosed to reimburse you for the cost of returning these goods.
>
> Mr Campbell will be contacting you again very soon, but if I can be of further assistance please telephone me.
>
> Yours sincerely
>
>
> JONATHAN PROCTOR
> General Manager

Omission of reference or date

> **Comlon International plc**
>
> Comlon House West Street London SW1Y 2AR
>
> tel: 0181 302 0261
> telex: Comlond 888941   telemessages: Comlond London SW1   fax: 0181 302 4169
>
>
> Mr David Simonson
> Programme Secretary
> London Toy Association
> 28 Fleet Street
> LONDON
> EC4 9HY
>
> Dear Mr Simonson

A successful approach

You will be successful in the Manuscript Transcription examination if you:

1 read through the entire paper and identify with the practical situation in which you are working

2 appreciate the overall theme running through the paper by noting the links and connections between assignments

3 follow instructions

4 transcribe an accurate interpretation of the employer's meaning

5 include all relevant details

6 display work consistently and appropriately

7 check and proofread carefully

8 ensure all documents are mailable

Unit 5

Complete examination papers

By the end of this unit you will be able to:

- *integrate the knowledge gained from working through units 1–4*

- *approach the examination with confidence*

- *apply the knowledge acquired to achieve a PASS in this examination*

PSC Examination December 1994

Now it is time to analyse a complete examination paper. Included here you will find the following sections:

- *The Instruction Sheet and the complete examination paper.*

- *Marked Answers.* A candidate's completed work on this paper shows where marks have been lost in each assignment.

- *Examiner's Comments.* The examiner discusses the candidate's work and gives the final percentage and result.

- *How marks could have been saved.* The examiner looks at each assignment and comments on marks which should not have been lost, marks which could have made a big difference to the final result.

DECEMBER SERIES 1994

**PRIVATE SECRETARY'S CERTIFICATE
EXAMINATION**

COMMUNICATION – TRANSCRIPTION – MANUSCRIPT

WEDNESDAY 7 DECEMBER 1994 – 1400 to 1615

————

Instructions to Candidates

*(a) The time allowed for this examination is **2** hours **15** minutes.*

*(b) Candidates must be allowed **15** minutes to study these instructions and the examination paper before commencing the transcription.*

(c) Candidates must read the examination paper carefully to find the necessary information to complete the assignments.

*(d) The time allowed for transcription is **2** hours.*

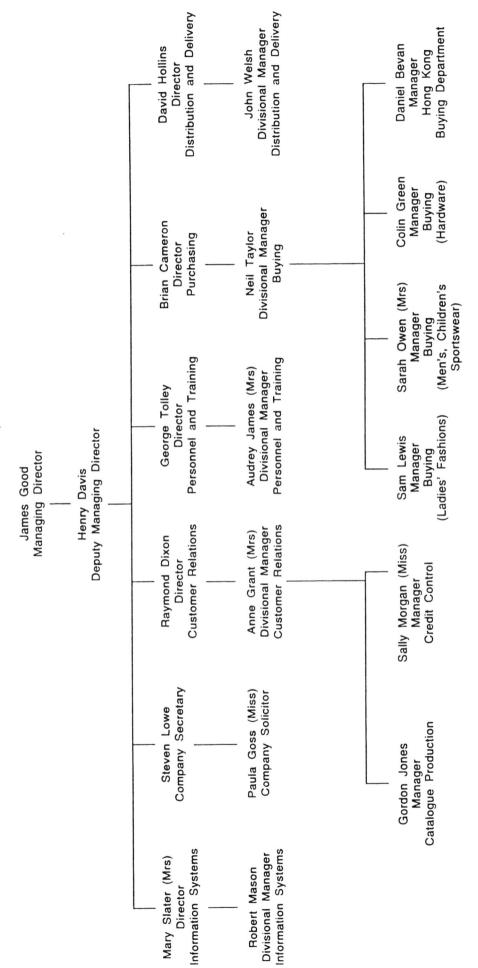

COMLON INTERNATIONAL plc

James Good
Managing Director

Henry Davis
Deputy Managing Director

Mary Slater (Mrs)
Director
Information Systems

Robert Mason
Divisional Manager
Information Systems

Steven Lowe
Company Secretary

Paula Goss (Miss)
Company Solicitor

Raymond Dixon
Director
Customer Relations

Anne Grant (Mrs)
Divisional Manager
Customer Relations

Sally Morgan (Miss)
Manager
Credit Control

Gordon Jones
Manager
Catalogue Production

George Tolley
Director
Personnel and Training

Audrey James (Mrs)
Divisional Manager
Personnel and Training

Brian Cameron
Director
Purchasing

Neil Taylor
Divisional Manager
Buying

Sam Lewis
Manager
Buying
(Ladies' Fashions)

Sarah Owen (Mrs)
Manager
Buying
(Men's, Children's
Sportswear)

Colin Green
Manager
Buying
(Hardware)

David Hollins
Director
Distribution and Delivery

John Welsh
Divisional Manager
Distribution and Delivery

Daniel Bevan
Manager
Hong Kong
Buying Department

PSC/SCLS/SCOT Dec 94

2

INFORMATION FOR CANDIDATES

The candidate works for Robert Mason, Divisional Manager, Information Systems, Comlon International plc.

Mr Mason likes his letters to be completed in the following way

ROBERT MASON
Divisional Manager
Information Systems

An organisation chart showing senior departmental relationships appears opposite. You will also need the following information

Paul Chan
Head of Buying Department

Comlon International plc
15 Harbour Road
Hong Kong

CONSISTENT USE OF ANY STYLE OF PUNCTUATION AND LAYOUT IS ACCEPTABLE

NOTES

(a) Envelopes are **NOT** required.

(b) Candidates must use Originator/Typist reference initials on each piece of work.

(c) Each piece of work must be dated with the date of the examination unless otherwise instructed.

(d) Arrange papers in assignment order in the bag-envelope provided.

(e) Unused examination material should **not** be returned.

(f) The use of standard English dictionaries and cordless non-programmable calculators is permitted. Candidates whose first language is not English may use a bilingual dictionary.

Further instructions are given on each assignment.

ASSIGNMENT 1

Write a memo to Audrey James, Training about the PC Training Courses.

Tell her that the courses proved so popular this year I propose to run similar courses commencing March 1995. Enclose copy of draft programme for her information and comment, also copy of my article about the future development of PCs. I hope the article will be published in the next edition of the house magazine. Also tell her

1. The courses will include 2 follow-up courses for those who attended this year.
2. Voice-activated PCs require special dictating techniques. Maybe we should discuss courses in dictating techniques for managers; should be introduced gradually over next few years, not wait until such PCs are standard – could result in better production from those still using shorthand and audio – may we discuss these suggestions further?

2

ASSIGNMENT 2

Please type draft programme for PC Training Courses 1995 – use headed paper. Type the aim of the Course, duration and dates on separate lines under the appropriate Course Number.

COURSE 1   2 day course 0900-1600 Saturdays 4 March and 11 March. Using a PC – A course for beginners

2   Everyday DOS (for those who have completed the first course) Saturday 18 March 0900-1630 1 day

3   Advanced DOS (This course follows on from the basic course Everyday DOS.) 0900-1630 Saturday 25 March   1 day

4   Saturdays 1 April and 8 April Word for Windows 2 days 0900-1600 (This course offers an intensive introduction to the features and facilities of Windows. A basic knowledge of computers and familiarity with a computer keyboard is assumed.)

3

ASSIGNMENT 3

Please re-type as amended and add details of the models as shown

MEMORANDUM

TO   ALL SENIOR MANAGERS

FROM ROBERT MASON, DIVISIONAL MANAGER, INFORMATION SYSTEMS

DATE 7 DECEMBER 1994

REF   RM/WPP

NEW **laptop**/NOTEBOOKS

All next week I shall have in my department 4 demonstration models of the latest laptop notebooks. Managers are welcome to visit the department at any time to view and operate these models. *Members of my staff will be available to demonstrate the functions and answer questions.* Please telephone my secretary if you require further details.

NP

I give below details of the 4 models on display.

Model	Mbyte hard disk	Mbyte memory	Features
Travel Companion 50	200	8	Mono; Windows, roller-ball mouse
Travel Companion 40	200	8	Colour screen; Windows
Compacta 20	40	2	Mono; can be upgraded to 4 RAM
Carrimate 25	80	4	Mono; lightweight carrying case

between 1000 and 1200 or from 1400 to 1600 Monday to Friday

ASSIGNMENT 4

Send a letter to Paul Chan, Hong Kong

Dear Paul - WORD PROCESSING SYSTEMS

I refer to your FAX 0824171. I am pleased to hear that you expect to visit us soon. Please call me when you are in London so that we can arrange to have lunch and discuss your word processing needs further.

Continue with extracts from my article (copy attached) on Word Processing as indicated by numbers but do not number paragraphs. Type only the words between the square brackets. Run ② and ③ together as one paragraph and do the same with ④ and ⑤. End the letter as shown below.

I look forward to meeting you. I shall be pleased to help in any way I can.

Yours sincerely

5

CONTINUED ON NEXT PAGE

FOR USE WITH ASSIGNMENT 4 ONLY

HERE'S THE WORD ON WORD PROCESSING

from ROBERT MASON, DIVISIONAL MANAGER, INFORMATION SYSTEMS

(1) [The first word processors were very simple. All the program had to do was imitate the action of an electric typewriter and add the boon of editing capacity.]

There were some weird and wonderful attempts at producing word processing programs. One did not use the space bar and substituted alt S instead. It was not a great success. Another made the claim that it would print out scientific symbols, which was true, but not of a science known to man.

(2) [In the beginning the dedicated word processor made all the running.] The difference between using a properly set up dedicated word processor and struggling along with software on a CP/M machine was the difference between driving a Robin and a Mercedes. Yet we struggled because anything was better than using a typewriter.

True, the typewriter had improved since Mark Twain started writing novels on it. (He later invested his fortune in typewriters and lost the lot.) After re-typing a page three times on a typewriter you would probably say "Let it go." With word processing programs, no matter how basic, you could revise, revise and then revise again without having to type out the whole page. This led to improved writing. Whatever the greybeards say, writing is better today than it was 15 years ago.

The first novelist to spot the advantage of the word processor was Len Deighton who used one to write BOMBER. After him came the deluge.

(3) [But [In the past few years word processing programs have improved so that they are now better than dedicated word processors.] Some wellknown companies which came to glory with these machines are now in serious trouble.

/that Where do word processing programs stand at present? (4) [The main line programs are so powerful ⟨they are, in effect and in fact, minor desktop publishing programs.] indexing programs and nearly everything else programs. On them you can create documents – writing is but part of the process – which are up to publishing standard and which contain complex mathematical tables and graphs which change in sympathy with the original figures.

There are some problems with these modern wonders. (5) [However it has been said The Pareto principle applies that only 20 per cent of the users use 80 per cent of the features and 80 per cent of the users only bother with 20 per cent of the features.] If you demonstrate word processing programs to supposedly sophisticated users you get a chorus of "I didn't know it could do that." The three most important but under-used facilities on a word processing program are macros, style sheets and spell checkers.

A macro saves you drudgery and duplication of effort on standard tasks. Style sheets give you company layouts – letters, fax, often used forms – available on call with one or two keys for as long as you want them. Spell checkers are different. All they do is see that a word spelt one way in your document exists in the memory of the computer. It cannot distinguish between.

(6) [It is important to decide what you need and then to find the equipment and programs which suit your requirements.]

6

ASSIGNMENT 5

Please re-type as amended

ARTICLE FOR HOUSE MAGAZINE

TAKE A LETTER — VOICE-ACTIVATED PC

distinctly

computer

My secretary sat in front of a laptop with a microphone held to the corner of
her mouth by a headband. She spoke ~~in a clear voice~~ with each word *clearly* separated
from the next. She dictated the commas, fullstops and paragraphs. As she
spoke her words appeared on the screen in synchronisation with her voice.

She dictated happily away until there were 200 words on the screen. ~~Even~~
she is new to her
Though she is not an absolute beginner ~~she is fairly new to~~ the system and ~~only~~
managed about 40 words a minute. More experienced users have exceeded normal
copy typing speed.

she only

~~This means of dictating is called 'discrete utterance'.~~ It merely means that
there is a clearly defined pause between each word. Eventually this slight
problem will also be solved and the computer will one day be able to recognise
run-on speech as, in the same way, it will one day be able ~~to recognise running
writing. But~~ (Dictating in a slightly staccato way is not difficult) ~~The ability
to dictate into a computer has been around for a long time.~~

What has allowed voice recognition systems to get beyond the area of
interesting experimentation to commercial use has been the phenomenal increase
in speed, power and memory capacity of the modern personal computer. This
power and speed is essential.

If you dictate a word into a computer ~~there~~ (are) two separate levels of action
required. The first is for the computer to look up the word in its list of
acceptable words and that can mean a very substantial vocabulary indeed.   If
the program finds the word it will be displayed on the screen for the dictator
to approve.

but a
A major problem arises because so many English words are pronounced in the
same way but spelled differently. ~~For example, the computer has to guess~~
whether the dictator requires the word two, too or to. ~~The computer can only
make the selection by studying the context in which the word appears.~~ To
handle this the computer needs an analytical engine - call it expert system or
artificial intelligence if you prefer - which will look at the word in context
~~and make a shrewd guess at the right spelling.~~ It has to do this at a speed
which is close to instantaneous so that the dictator does not have to wait to
see that the correct decision has been made. ~~Although the theory has been
known for a long time the power to drive such computation has not existed. Now
it does with the advent of 486-driven personal computers with large memories
at a reasonable price.~~

It is important to understand that the system is not a substitute for all
typing. It is a substitute for dictation. ~~and~~ Typing ~~and~~ is much quicker and
much less prone to mistakes. The dictator sees the results on the screen and
can use macros ~~- pre-written paragraphs and forms -~~ to call up all types of
work and add, amend and improve. The importance cannot be measured by merely
comparing such a system with a typist's speed; it has to be judged over the
NP whole process. [I can foresee the day when this system is standard on most new
office computers.

*The computer has to make the selection by studying the
context in which the word appears.*

ASSIGNMENT 6

Please reply to this letter. Make the points shown below

BOUTIQUE EXPRESS SA
117 rue de Seine
75008 Paris
France

5 December 1994

Mr Robert Mason
Divisional Manager, Information Systems
Comlon International plc
West Street
LONDON   SW1Y 2AR

Dear Mr Mason

PC TRAINING COURSES

In March this year I followed a course for beginners organised by your
department and I have found the skill and knowledge I acquired extremely useful.

I have been seconded to Boutique-Express until the end of January 1995 but I
have been asked whether I would be prepared to stay until the end of February.

As I am very anxious to take a more advanced PC course please let me know
whether you intend to run further courses in 1995 and whether I will be
eligible to attend as I have been absent from the London office for more than
six months.

I should be grateful if you would reply as soon as possible as your information
could influence my decision about the date of my return.

A letter addressed to me care of the Directeur, Monsieur Jean Bouchon, will be
passed to me.

Yours sincerely

CLARE WATSON
Catalogue Consultant

1. Pleased she found the course useful
2. As last ~~courses~~ courses proved popular, similar courses are proposed for 1995. Enclose draft programme and mention follow-up courses.
3. She could stay in France until end of Feb. as courses begin 18 March
4. If she telephones on return to H.O. I'll arrange for her to attend an advanced course as she needs

Marked answers

Assignment 1

Comlon International plc

Comlon House West Street London SW1Y 2AR

Paper X   −1

tel: 0181 302 0261
telex: Comlond 888941   telemessages: Comlond London SW1   fax: 0181 302 4169

MEMORANDUM

To   :   Audrey James Divisional Manager   −1
                 Personnel and Training

From   :   Robert Mason – title?   −1

Ref   :   RM/HC

Date   :   7 December 1994

                                        Heading   −1

Please be informed that the courses proved so popular this year   −1
I proposed to run similar courses commencing on March 1995.   −1 −1
Enclosed is a copy of draft programme for your information and   −1
comment, also copy of my article about the future development
of PCs. I hope the article will be published in the next
edition of the house magazine.

I also like to tell you that the courses will include 2 follow-   −1
up courses for those who attended this year.

Voice-activated PCs require special dictating techniques.
Maybe we should discuss courses in dictating techniques for
managers; it should be introduced gradually over next few   −1 −1
years, not wait until such PCs are standard-result could be   −1
better production from those still using shorthand/audio.   −1

I would like to discuss about these suggestions further with   −1
you.

Kind Regards   X

Enc −1

                        Total Penalties = 15

Assignment 2

Comlon International plc

Comlon House West Street London SW1Y 2AR

Display   −1

tel: 0181 302 0261
telex: Comlond 888941   telemessages: Comlond London SW1   fax: 0181 302 4169

Draft   −1

*** PC TRAINING COURSES 1995 ***

<u>COURSE</u>   <u>DURATION</u>   <u>DATES</u>

1   2 days   Saturdays
Using a PC −   0900−1600   4 March and 11 March

A course for beginners

2   1 day   Saturday
Everyday DOS   0900−1630   18 March

(for those who have completed the first course)

3   1 day   Saturday
Advanced DOS   0900−1630   25 March

(This course follows on from the basic course Everyday DOS)

4   2 days   Saturdays
Word for (w)indows   0900−1600   1 April and 8 April   *−1*

(This course (offer) an extensive introduction to the features   *−1*
and facilities of (w)indows. A basic knowledge of computers
and familiarity with a computer keyboard is assumed.)

Ref/Date   −2

Total Penalties = 6

Assignment 3

MEMORANDUM

To   :   All Senior Managers

From   :   Robert Mason, Divisional Manager,
                Information Systems

Ref   :   RM/HC

Date   :   7 December 1994

NEW LAPTOP (NOTE BOOKS)   −|

All next week I shall have in my department 4 (demostration)   −| −|
(madels) of the latest laptop notebooks. Managers are welcome to
visit the department at any time between 1000 and 1200 or from
1400 to 1600 Monday to Friday to view and operate these models.
Members of my staff will be available to (demostrate) the   −|
(function) and answer questions.   −|

I give below details of the 4 models on display. Please
telephone my secretary if you require further details.

Model	Mbyte hand disk	Mbyte memory	Features
Travel Companion 50	200	8	Mono; Windows, (rdller) − ball mouse
Travel Companion 40	200	8	Colour screen; Windows
Compacta 20	40	2	Mono; can be upgraded to 4 RAM
Carrimate 25	80	4	Mono; lightweight carrying case

−| −|

Total Penalties = 7

Comlon International plc

Comlon House West Street London SW1Y 2AR

tel: 0181 302 0261
telex: Comlond 888941   telemessages: Comlond London SW1   fax: 0181 302 4169

RM/HC

7 December 1994

Paul Chan
Head of Buying Department
Comlon International plc
15 Harbour Road
Hong Kong

Dear Mr Chan

WORD PROCESSING SYSTEMS

I refer to your FAX 0824171. I am pleased to fear that you
expect to visit us soon. Please call me when you are in London
so that we can arrange to have lunch and discuss your word
processing needs further.

The first word processors were very simple. All the program
had to do was imitate the action of an electric typewriter and
add the boon of editing capacity. In the beginning the
dedicated word processor made all the running. But in the past
few years word processing programs have improved so that they
are now better than dedicated word processors.

The main line programs are so powerful that they are minor
desktop publishing programs. However it has been said that
only 20 percent of the users use 80 percent of the features and
0 percent of the users only bother with 20 percent of the
features. It is important to decide what you need and then to
find the equipment and programs which suit your requirements.

I look forward to meeting you. I shall be pleased to help in
any way I can.

Yours sincerely

....
Robert Mason
Divisional Manager (Information Systems)

Total Penalties = 10

Assignment 5

ARTICLE FOR HOUSE MAGAZINE   −|

TAKE A LETTER − VOICE − ACTIVATED PC

My secretary sat in front of a laptop computer with a
microphone held to the corner of her mouth by a headband.
She spoke districtly with each word clearly separated from   −|
the next. She dictated the commas, fullstops and paragraphs. −|
As she spoke her word appeared on the screen in synchronisat-   −|
ion with her voice.   −|

She dictated until there were 200 words on the screen. Thought −|
she is not an absolute beginner the system is raw to her and   −|
she only managed about 40 words a minute. More experienced
users have exceeded normal copy typing speed.

What has allowed voice recognition systems to get beyond the
area of interesting experimentation to commercial use has been
the phenomenal increase in speed, power and memory capacity of   −|
the modern personal computer. This power and speed is
essential.

If you dictated a word into a computer two separate levels of   −|
action are required. The first is for the computer to look up
the word in its list of acceptable words and that can mean a
very substantial vocabulary indeed. If the program finds the
word it will be displayed on the screen for the dictator to
approve.

Dictating in a slightly staccato way is not difficult but a
major problem arises because so many English words are
pronounce in the same way but spelled differently. The   −|
computer has to make the selection by studying the context in
which the word appears. It has to do this at a speed which is
close to instantaneous so that the dictator does not have to
wait to see that the correct decision has been made.

It is important to understand that the system is not a
substitute for all typing. It is a substitute for dictation.
Typing is much quicker and much less prone to mistakes. The
dictator sees the results on the screen and can use macros to
call up all types of word and add, amend and improve. The
importance cannot be measured by merely comparing such a system
with a typist's speed; it has to be judge over the whole   −|
process.

I can foresee the day when this system is standard on most new
office computers.

Req / Date   −2

Total Penalties = 12

Assignment 6

Comlon International plc

Comlon House West Street London SW1Y 2AR

tel: 0181 302 0261
telex: Comlond 888941   telemessages: Comlond London SW1   fax: 0181 302 4169

RM/HC

7 December 1994

Miss Clare Watson   ?

BOUTIQUE EXPRESS SA
117 rue de Seine
75008 Paris
France

Dear Miss Clare

PC TRAINING COURSES

I am please to know that you found the course is useful to you
and am writing to thank you for your letter which is dated on
5 December.

I wish to let you know that Saturday courses proved popular.
Similar course are proposed for 1995. Please find enclosed
the draft programme and mention follow-up courses.

You had mention about staying in France so please stay there
until/end of February as courses begin 18 March.

If you telephones on return to H.O. I'll arrange for you to
attend an advanced course as you needs.

We hope to hear from you soon.

Thanking you.

Yours sincerely

Total Penalties = 17

....
Robert Mason
Divisional Manager (Information Systems)

Examiner's comments

Penalties:	Assignment 1	15	
	Assignment 2	6	
	Assignment 3	7	
	Assignment 4	10	
	Assignment 5	12	
	Assignment 6	17	
	Total Penalties	67	
	Final Mark	33%	RESULT: FAIL

Apart from the obvious typographical errors throughout this candidate's work, there are also numerous grammatical errors. Many of these errors could have been avoided by more careful preparation prior to transcription and by more thoughtful proofreading.

However, many of the errors made were 'mechanical' errors, ie marks have been lost because of faulty display and layout. Although such errors may have been made in earlier attempts, candidates should really not be making such errors at the time of the examination. They are marks which could have been saved.

With a final result of 33%, this candidate needed to save only 17 more marks to be awarded a pass.

How marks could have been saved

Assignment 1 – 6 penalties could be avoided:

Assignment 1

Comlon International plc

Comlon House West Street London SW1Y 2AR   ~~Paper X~~ -1

tel: 0181 302 0261
telex: Comlond 888941   telemessages: Comlond London SW1   fax: 0181 302 4169

MEMORANDUM

To   :   Audrey James Divisional Manager   -1
                Personnel and ⌣Training

From   :   Robert Mason – ~~title~~?   -1

Ref   :   RM/HC

Date   :   7 December 1994

                                              Heading   -1   ← A heading has not been composed.

(Please be informed) that the courses proved so popular this year   -1
I propos(ed) to run similar courses commencing (on) March 1995.   -1 -1
Enclosed is a‿copy of draft programme for your information and   -1
comment, also‿copy of my article about the future development
of PCs. I hope the article will be published in the next
edition of the house magazine.

(I also like to tell you) that the courses will include 2 follow-   -1
up courses for those who attended this year.

Voice-activated PCs require special dictating techniques.
Maybe we should discuss courses in dictating techniques for
managers; (it) should be introduced gradually over‿the next few   -1 -1
years, not wait until such PCs are (standard-result) could be   -1
better production from those still using ~~shorthand~~/audio.   -1

I would like to discuss (about) these suggestions further with   -1
you.

Kind Regards X

Enc -1

                    Total Penalties = 15

Right-hand margin annotations:

← Letterheaded paper has been used instead of plain bond.

← The sender's designation has not been shown.

← The dash has not been displayed correctly (with a space before and after it).

← 'Kind Regards' is unnecessary.

← 'Enc' has not been indicated.

Notes

1 It has been assumed that the candidate has used a house style for displaying memos so this has not been penalised. However, the layout used for the headings is not at all attractive, with unequal spacing before and after the colons. Why are the colons necessary?

2 'Please be informed' and 'I also like to tell you that' are very long-winded and old-fashioned. Why not simply get straight to the point?

123

Assignment 2 – 5 penalties could be avoided:

Assignment 2

Comlon International plc

Comlon House West Street London SW1Y 2AR

tel: 0181 302 0261
telex: Comlond 888941   telemessages: Comlond London SW1   fax: 0181 302 4169

Display   –1

Draft   –1

*** PC TRAINING COURSES 1995 ***

<u>COURSE</u>	<u>DURATION</u>	<u>DATES</u>
1	2 days	Saturdays
Using a PC –	0900-1600	4 March and 11 March
A course for beginners		
2	1 day	Saturday
Everyday DOS	0900-1630	18 March
(for those who have completed the first course)		
3	1 day	Saturday
Advanced DOS	0900-1630	25 March
(This course follows on from the basic course Everyday DOS)		
4	2 days	Saturdays
Word for windows	0900-1600	1 April and 8 April

–1

(This course offer an extensive introduction to the features
and facilities of windows. A basic knowledge of computers
and familiarity with a computer keyboard is assumed.)

–1

Ref/Date   –2

Total Penalties = 6

← Letterheaded paper has been used instead of plain bond.

← The candidate has not indicated that this is a draft.

← The overall display of this programme is very poor and not in accordance with the employer's instructions to 'Type the aim of the course, duration and dates on separate lines under the appropriate Course Number'. Also, even if columns would have been appropriate, the centred main heading and centred column headings are inconsistent with the blocked style letterhead.

← The candidate has only been penalised once for typing 'windows' without an initial capital.

← The reference and date should be shown on all documents.

Assignment 3 – 4 penalties could be avoided:

```
                                        Assignment 3

MEMORANDUM

To     :       All Senior Managers

From   :       Robert Mason, Divisional Manager,
               Information Systems

Ref    :       RM/HC

Date   :       7 December 1994


NEW LAPTOP NOTE BOOKS                                        -1

All next week I shall have in my department 4 demostration   -1
madels of the latest laptop notebooks.  Managers are welcome to
visit the department at any time between 1000 and 1200 or from
1400 to 1600 Monday to Friday to view and operate these models.
Members of my staff will be available to demonstrate the     -1
function and answer questions.                               -1

I give below details of the 4 models on display.  Please
telephone my secretary if you require further details.

    Model       Mbyte       Mbyte       Features
                hand disk   memory

Travel Companion
50              200         8           Mono; Windows,
                                        rdller - ball mouse   -1  -1

Travel Companion
40              200         8           Colour screen;
                                        Windows

Compacta 20     40          2           Mono; can be upgraded
                                        to 4 RAM

Carrimate 25    80          4           Mono; lightweight
                                        carrying case


              Total Penalties = 7
```

← 'NOTEBOOKS' is displayed correctly on the examination paper.

← 'demonstration' is also spelled correctly on the paper. (This has only been penalised once although the candidate misspelled it twice.)

← The columns are poorly displayed again, with centred column headings. This has not been penalised, although the display of the model name in column one has lost a mark unnecessarily.

← The hyphenated word 'rollerball' is clearly indicated on the manuscript.

Assignment 4 – 5 penalties could be avoided:

Assignment 4

Comlon International plc

Comlon House West Street London SW1Y 2AR

tel: 0181 302 0261
telex: Comlond 888941   telemessages: Comlond London SW1   fax: 0181 302 4169

RM/HC

7 December 1994

Mr
Paul Chan   -1   ← A courtesy title should
Head of Buying Department   always be included for
Comlon International plc   addressees of letters.
15 Harbour Road
Hong Kong

Dear Mr Chan   -1   ← The employer clearly
                                                                                        wrote 'Dear Paul'.
WORD PROCESSING SYSTEMS

I refer to your FAX 0824171. I am pleased to fear that you   -1
expect to visit us soon. Please call me when you are in London
so that we can arrange to have lunch and discuss your word
processing needs further.

        The first word processors were very simple. All the program
        had to do was imitate the action of an electric typewriter and
NP   add the boon of editing capacity. // In the beginning the   -1   ← The instructions clearly
        dedicated word processor made all the running. But in the past   -1   asked for points 2 and
        few years word processing programs have improved so that they   3 to be run together as
        are now better than dedicated word processors.   one paragraph. Point 6
                                                                                        should have been a
        The main line programs are so powerful that they are minor   -1   separate paragraph.
        desktop publishing programs. However it has been said that
only 20 percent of the users use 80 percent of the features and   -1   ← 'per cent' is clearly
        0 percent of the users only bother with 20 percent of the   -1   shown as two words
NP   features. // It is important to decide what you need and then to   -1   on the paper.
        find the equipment and programs which suit your requirements.

        I look forward to meeting you. I shall be pleased to help in
        any way I can.

        Yours sincerely

....   X   -1   ← The letter has not been
Robert Mason   completed as stated on
Divisional Manager (Information Systems)   Total Penalties = 10   the instruction sheet.

Assignment 5 – 3 penalties could be avoided:

```
                                          Assignment 5


ARTICLE FOR HOUSE MAGAZINE                                    - |

TAKE A LETTER - VOICE - ACTIVATED PC

My secretary sat in front of a laptop computer with a
microphone held to the corner of her mouth by a headband.     - |
She spoke districtly with each word clearly separated from
the next.  She dictated the commas, fullstops and paragraphs. - |
As she spoke her word appeared on the screen in synchronisat-    - |
ion with her voice.

She dictated until there were 200 words on the screen.  Thought  - |
she is not an absolute beginner the system is raw to her and   - |
she only managed about 40 words a minute.  More experienced
users have exceeded normal copy typing speed.

What has allowed voice recognition systems to get beyond the
area of interesting experimentation to commercial use has been
the phenomenal increase in speed, power and memory capacity of  - |
the modern personal computer.  This power and speed is
essential.

If you dictated a word into a computer two separate levels of   - |
action are required.  The first is for the computer to look up
the word in its list of acceptable words and that can mean a
very substantial vocabulary indeed.  If the program finds the
word it will be displayed on the screen for the dictator to
approve.

Dictating in a slightly staccato way is not difficult but a
major problem arises because so many English words are
pronounce in the same way but spelled differently.  The       - |
computer has to make the selection by studying the context in
which the word appears.  It has to do this at a speed which is
close to instantaneous so that the dictator does not have to
wait to see that the correct decision has been made.

It is important to understand that the system is not a
substitute for all typing.  It is a substitute for dictation.
Typing is much quicker and much less prone to mistakes.  The
dictator sees the results on the screen and can use macros to
call up all types of word and add, amend and improve.  The
importance cannot be measured by merely comparing such a system
with a typist's speed; it has to be judge over the whole        - |
process.

I can foresee the day when this system is standard on most new
office computers.



Ref/Date    -2
                   Total Penalties = 12
```

← 'VOICE-ACTIVATED' was clearly hyphenated in the employer's manuscript. This candidate has confused the hyphen and dash throughout this work.

← If in doubt, do not divide words at line-ends. It alters the pronunciation of the word to type 'synchronisat' on one line and 'ion' on the next.

There are several careless errors which could have been avoided with more careful preparation. In particular, the word 'raw' in the second paragraph does not make sense – it should be 'new'.

Assignment 6 – 7 penalties could be avoided:

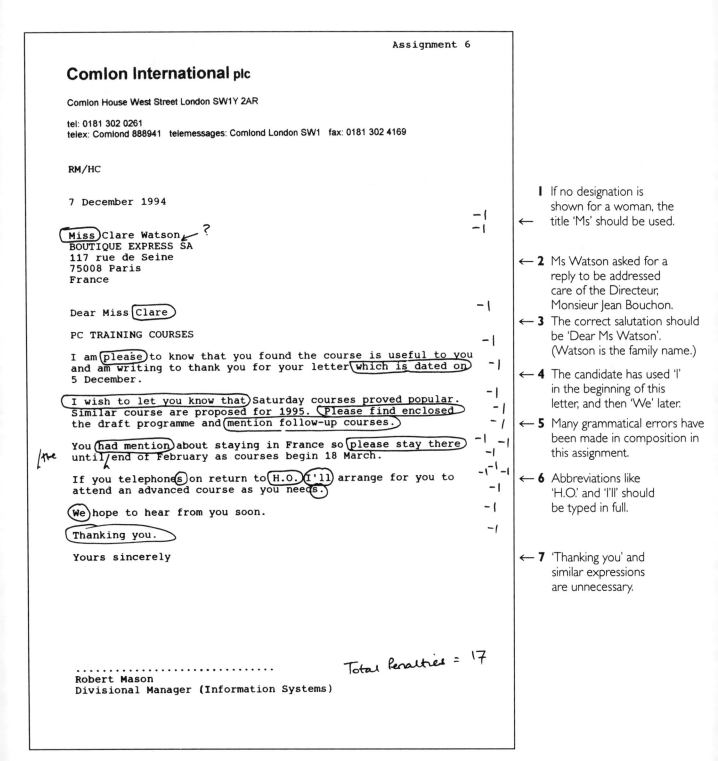

Conclusion

As you will see, many of these comments mostly concern 'mechanical' features relating to general display and layout. These errors are particularly disappointing because prior to the examination sufficient practice should have been gained so that plain bond is automatically used for memos, letterheaded paper for letters, etc. Similarly, marks should not be lost for using the incorrect salutation, displaying the employer's name incorrectly, not indicating an enclosure, omitting the reference and date. By the time of the examination, correct production of all these things should be automatic. Examiners find it very disappointing when they have to deduct marks for this type of error, because these marks often mean the difference between pass and fail.

In this example, the candidate was awarded only 33%. Although only 17 more marks were required for a PASS, we have actually seen at least 30 marks which could easily have been saved.

It has to be stressed again that this result could, and should, have been a PASS. What is needed is:

- thoughtful preparation in the months/weeks prior to the examination
- good use of the 15 minutes' reading time to read, prepare and understand the work
- use of initiative during the examination
- thoughtful transcription without rushing
- careful proofreading on completion of each task

After studying the examination paper, the sample script and the examiner's comments and final report, you are advised to work through the paper yourself. In this way you can put into practice all the tips you have learned so far. Only when you are satisfied with your work should you compare it with the check copies on pages 182–187. It is stressed that these are check copies – they show work which the examiner would have considered distinction level. Please remember that in this examination there can be no 'model answers' – only work which interprets the employer's meaning correctly, accurately and appropriately. Also included on pages 180–181 is the Examiner's Report so that you can learn from mistakes made by other candidates in this examination.

SSC Examination – December 1994

We will now take a look at another complete examination paper, this time from the SSC. You should now be able to work through the paper by yourself, but you are given advice to help you.

Study the Instruction Sheet and the complete examination paper carefully. Read through each assignment first and then consider the advice provided.

Before you begin transcribing the assignments, refer back to page 104 where you were given advice about 'A Successful Approach'.

When you have attempted all the assignments, refer to the check copies on pages 188–193. Please remember, however, that these are merely check copies and not 'model answers'.

Good luck!

DECEMBER SERIES 1994

**SECRETARIAL STUDIES CERTIFICATE
EXAMINATION**

COMMUNICATION – TRANSCRIPTION – MANUSCRIPT

WEDNESDAY 30 NOVEMBER 1994 – 1400 to 1615

_____

Instructions to Candidates

*(a) The time allowed for this examination is **2** hours **15** minutes.*

*(b) Candidates must be allowed **15** minutes to study these instructions and the examination paper before commencing the transcription.*

(c) Candidates must read the examination paper carefully to find the necessary information to complete the assignments.

*(d) The time allowed for transcription is **2** hours.*

131

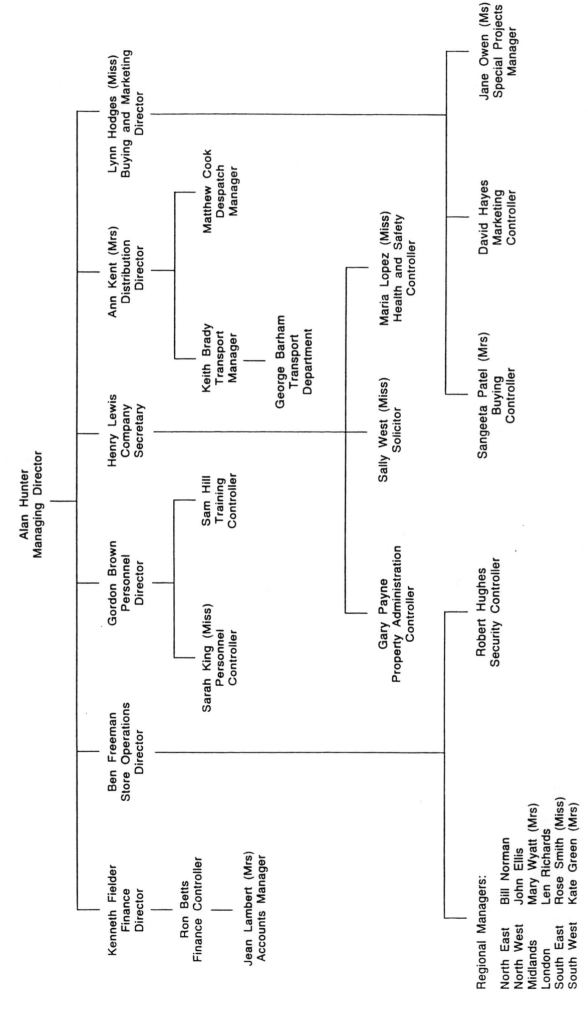

COMLON INTERNATIONAL plc

Alan Hunter
Managing Director

Kenneth Fielder
Finance
Director

Ben Freeman
Store Operations
Director

Gordon Brown
Personnel
Director

Henry Lewis
Company
Secretary

Ann Kent (Mrs)
Distribution
Director

Lynn Hodges (Miss)
Buying and Marketing
Director

Ron Betts
Finance Controller

Jean Lambert (Mrs)
Accounts Manager

Sarah King (Miss)
Personnel
Controller

Sam Hill
Training
Controller

Keith Brady
Transport
Manager

Matthew Cook
Despatch
Manager

George Barham
Transport
Department

Gary Payne
Property Administration
Controller

Sally West (Miss)
Solicitor

Maria Lopez (Miss)
Health and Safety
Controller

Robert Hughes
Security Controller

Sangeeta Patel (Mrs)
Buying
Controller

David Hayes
Marketing
Controller

Jane Owen (Ms)
Special Projects
Manager

Regional Managers:

North East	Bill Norman
North West	John Ellis
Midlands	Mary Wyatt (Mrs)
London	Len Richards
South East	Rose Smith (Miss)
South West	Kate Green (Mrs)

SSC/FCLS/FCOT Dec 94

INFORMATION FOR CANDIDATES

The candidate works for Ben Freeman, Store Operations Director, Comlon International plc.

Mr Freeman likes his letters to be completed in the following way

BEN FREEMAN
Store Operations Director

An organisation chart showing senior departmental relationships appears opposite. You will also need the following information

Alan Hunter	The Manager
c/o Hotel Syon	
	Wellington Hotel
118 rue de Vaugirard	West Street
07006 Paris	London
France	SW1Y 2BX

CONSISTENT USE OF ANY STYLE OF PUNCTUATION AND LAYOUT IS ACCEPTABLE

NOTES

(a) Envelopes are **NOT** required.

(b) Candidates must use Originator/Typist reference initials on each piece of work.

(c) Each piece of work must be dated with the date of the examination unless otherwise instructed.

(d) Arrange papers in assignment order in the bag-envelope provided.

(e) Unused examination material should **not** be returned.

(f) The use of standard English dictionaries and cordless non-programmable calculators is permitted. Candidates whose first language is not English may use a bilingual dictionary.

Further instructions are given on each assignment.

© LCCI 1994

ASSIGNMENT 1

leave the salutation blank

Type a letter to the Managing Director. He is touring Europe so send the letter % Hotel Syon

c/o ws 118 Rue de Vaugirard (Paris 07006). Tell him I have concluded arrangements for the conference for Regional Managers (give dates). Enclose an outline programme, a copy of which has been sent to each manager. A detailed programme will be enclosed in the conference wallet which will also contain copies of handouts

supplied

by the conference speakers, also information about the social events which have been arranged.

Tell him I was pleased to hear that he will be back from France in time to attend the Reception and Dinner in the Waterloo Room of the Wellington Hotel on Friday 27 Jan. He will see from the memo I have sent to all Regional Managers (enclose a copy) Mr Nigel Baker, Man. Dir. of FRESHGLO PRODUCTS INC has accepted my invitation to be the Guest Speaker. Thank him very much for agreeing to propose

c/o the Vote of Thanks and say that you will send him biographical details about Mr Baker nearer the date. *End in usual way.*

2

← Remember 'Tell him' is an instruction to you.

← The conference date is mentioned on the next assignment.

← Change the pronoun 'he' to 'you'.

← Take care in composition of this sentence.

← Type this abbreviation, 'Managing Director', in full.

← 'Thank him' – 'him' refers to Mr Hunter. 'say that you will' – 'you' refers to the secretary.

Notes

1 Use correct paper for this letter, and remember the appropriate preliminary details. The Managing Director's name is shown on both the organisation chart and the Instruction Sheet, together with the address of the Hotel Syon.

2 Read these notes carefully first so that you understand the context of the letter.

3 Follow the employer's directions to leave the salutation blank so that he can handwrite this section.

4 Remember to paragraph appropriately.

5 Use the correct complimentary close and refer to the Instruction Sheet to check how your employer likes his letters to be completed.

6 Make a note to remember to include 'Enc' at the bottom.

Pointers

ASSIGNMENT 2

MEMORANDUM

TO   ALL REGIONAL MANAGERS

\# FROM BEN FREEMAN STORE OPERATIONS DIRECTOR

DATE 30 NOVEMBER 1994

REF   BF/

Please retype this memo as amended

(REGIONAL MANAGERS) ANNUAL CONFERENCE FOR ↓

~~This is to confirm that~~ **A** one day conference will be held in the Comlon
⁴/c Conference Centre on Saturday 28 January 1995. ~~which~~ all Regional Managers are
expected to attend.

Accommodation for the nights of Friday 27 January and Saturday 28 January has
been arranged at the Wellington Hotel, West Street. *The hotel* ~~which~~ is within walking
distance of Comlon House.

The conference includes all meals from dinner on Friday until Sunday breakfast.
Managers may check in to the hotel *at any time* ~~after 12~~ noon on Friday 27 January. Check-
out time on Sunday 29 January has been extended to 1800 to enable managers to
spend the day in London if they wish to do so.

A Reception and Dinner will be held in the Waterloo Room of the Wellington
⁴/c Hotel on Friday 27 January, 1900 for 1930. ~~at which~~ the Guest Speaker will be
Mr Nigel Baker, Managing Director, Freshglo Products Inc.

On Saturday 28 January a buffet supper will be served in the hotel between
1830 and 2000. Tickets have been obtained for the evening performance *on no date.* of
MISS SAIGON at the Theatre Royal, Drury Lane. As the number of tickets is
limited only those attending the conference may apply. Please complete the
tear-off slip and return to my secretary before 14 December.

NP [*Travelling expenses to and from the conference can be
claimed in the usual way.*

NP *The conference will cover a wide range of subjects
including future developments and marketing strategy.
An outline programme is enclosed for your information.*

- -

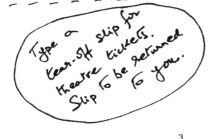

*Type a tear-off slip for
theatre tickets.
Slip to be returned
to you.*

3   OVER

← This tells you the
   information which
   should be included on
   the tear-off slip, ie
   whether managers
   want a ticket to attend
   MISS SAIGON.

← Make a note to
   remember 'Enc'.

← For a tear-off slip the
   unspaced hyphens
   should go from edge to
   edge of the paper.

← Do not forget details
   regarding return of the
   form. 'you' means
   Mr Freeman's secretary
   – give the full address.

Notes

1 Your employer has had a memo typed which he has
subsequently amended.

2 A tear-off slip must be included at the bottom of the
memo. By now you will have studied tear-off slips in your
Communication lessons. If necessary refer to the
guidelines in your textbook, *Communication for Business –
A Practical Approach*.

3 Draft the tear-off portion, considering the information
which your employer needs to know from each Regional
Manager.

4 Type this memo carefully, making all the amendments as
shown.

ASSIGNMENT 3

> Type the programme for the Conference for Regional Managers. The times and subjects of talks are given below. Please fill in names and designations of speakers and display effectively. You have an organisation chart to check designations of Comlon staff.

0900	Registration
0930	Welcome & introduction to Conference (I'll do that)
0945	Store security – from shoplifting to terrorism Robert Hughes, Security
1045	Freshglo Products – Video & Sales Presentation by Peter Hill, Freshglo Sales Manager
1130	Launching the new Freshglo range David Hayes, Marketing
1400	New developments in staff training Sarah King
1445	Healthy staff in a safe environment Health & Safety Controller
1530	Brains Trust – Discussion of current problems
	Panel – R Hughes, S King M Lopez, and me

> Insert Coffee at 1015, Tea 1600. Lunch will be in the Senior Management Dining Room at 1230

4

Pointers

← 'I'll do that' – who does this mean?

← Give the full title for Robert Hughes.

← Type the name of the company in full.

← Be consistent – use full names.

← Put pencil notes to remind you to insert these items.

Notes

1 This is a programme for the Conference referred to in previous assignments. Instructions regarding display are given in the balloon at the top of the assignment.

2 Compose an appropriate heading – perhaps the title of the conference on one line, followed by the date and the place where it will be held.

3 Type the programme in two columns, with the times on the left and the items on the right.

4 Each item has a title and most items show the name of the presenter. Use an attractive display which will be easy when referring to the programme.

5 Be consistent in display of each item throughout the programme.

6 Remember you can refer to the organisation chart if necessary.

ASSIGNMENT 4

Notes for Conference

Type these notes for my welcome and introduction to the Conference. Leave 3 or 4 lines between headings but type material under headings in single line-spacing

Welcome regional managers

Introduce new managers, *Bill Norman, Len Richards*

Congratulations and award to
   Rose Smith for best sales results 1994
   John Ellis, best window display

Introduce staff speakers - emphasise conference aims
List staff speakers please

Brief summary of achievements and problems
                  during the past year
   New stores in north west and south east
   National training awards
   Mention firebombs in Birmingham and
                              Manchester

Future developments
   Negotiations for new sites in Midlands
   Continual need for security vigilance
   Freshglo franchise, regional launches,
   hand out for use in each area

5   OVER

← Head this with the name of the conference again.

← Use the information in this balloon to compose a more appropriate second heading.

← Refer to the programme for names of the speakers representing Comlon.

Notes

1 These are the notes which your employer will use when welcoming delegates to the conference and in his introduction.

2 Display it attractively, perhaps emphasising the main items in some way. This will help Mr Freeman when referring to the notes.

3 Remember to space the items out as instructed.

ASSIGNMENT 5

Confirm the reservations for the conference with the Manager, Wellington Hotel, using our usual form (copy attached) for confirmation of reservations by telephone. I booked 11 rooms: for myself, our Regional Managers, and the conference speakers from Conlon. Freshglo representatives do not require overnight accommodation. No need to give full details of the Reception and Dinner or the Buffet Supper. Just add a note that detailed requirements for these are given in my letter ref... dated 1.9.94. Include the extended check-out on Sunday under special requirements. Accounts go to Accounts Department and enquiries come to you on extension 205.

7   OVER

Pointers

← The display for this letter is indicated on the attached outline letter. Remember to use letterheaded paper.

← Why not handwrite the appropriate details in the spaces on the outline letter?

Notes

1 These are notes and instructions to you, asking you to use the layout shown on the form provided to confirm reservations at the Wellington Hotel.

2 Refer to the form and note the headings given. When you read these notes consider where you will insert the details when typing out the letter to the hotel.

3 Before transcribing, write all the relevant details on the blank form. This will ensure that you insert everything in the correct place and that nothing is omitted.

4 Display the letter appropriately on letterheaded paper.

Pointers

```
                              TO BE USED BY CANDIDATES AS A
        Ref                   GUIDE FOR THE DISPLAY OF THE
                              LETTER REQUIRED IN ASSIGNMENT 5
        Date




        Dear                                                          ← 1

        CONFIRMATION OF RESERVATION

        I confirm the reservations made by telephone as follows       ← 2

        DATE(S)

        FUNCTION                                                      ← 3

        NUMBER OF BEDROOMS                                            ← 4

        NAMES OF GUESTS                                               ← 5



        MEALS                                                         ← 6




        SPECIAL REQUIREMENTS                                          ← 7



        ACCOUNTS TO                                                   ← 8


        ENQUIRIES TO                                                  ← 9


        Yours faithfully







                        6              CONTINUED ON NEXT PAGE
```

Key

1 Use an appropriate salutation.

2 Study the earlier memo to Regional Managers.

3 Function? This should be easy!

4 Mr Freeman tells you how many rooms he has booked.

5 The hotel will need full names of all the guests for their records.

6 Meals are mentioned in the memo to Regional Managers. Remember to add the note mentioned by Mr Freeman.

7 Again, you will find details of the extended checkout in the memo.

8 Mr Freeman gives you this information.

9 Mr Freeman's note says 'to you' – just type 'Mr Freeman's secretary . . . '

Pointers

ASSIGNMENT 6

CONFERENCE HANDOUT

FRESHGLO TOILETRIES

Single line-spacing
Type on headed paper/as handout for Regional Managers. Insert paragraphs as indicated by numbers on attached sheet. Do not type numbers

Comlon International plc is pleased to announce that agreement has been reached

⁴/₂ with Freshglo products Inc for an exclusive franchise to sell the new range of

Freshglo toiletries in ~~all~~ the/Comlon stores throughout the UK. *600*

⑤

The range of products includes

Hair shampoos, conditioners and styling mousses with specific cosmetic agents
to protect hair,/and preserve softness and shine. *maintain style,*

Face and hand creams and moisturisers with added sunscreen to protect delicate

skin and enhance texture. ①

Perfume, toilet water, after shave, body lotion, and talc deodorants in the

following fragrances. ②

③

Cosmetic packs containing mascara, lipstick, blusher and nail enamel in 2

varieties

④

The full range of FRESHGLO toiletries will be on sale at ~~all~~ Comlon Stores from *your local*

1 March 1995.

Free demonstrations and advice will be given.

8   **CONTINUED ON NEXT PAGE**

← The draft was originally double line spaced, but follow the instructions to retype it in single line spacing.

← These numbers are only for reference and should not be typed.

Pointers

FOR USE WITH ASSIGNMENT 6

① [Available in full fragrance range or fragrance-free]

(omit brackets)

② [Unscented deodorants are also available]

③ FOR HIM Serge, Corduroy, Tartan, Black Leather

FOR HER Chiffon, Silk, Velvet, Linen

④ AUTUMN for those who wear mainly reds, browns and oranges

SPRING for those who prefer to wear pastel shades

Caps ⑤ Freshglo products conform to the strict Conlon standards for producing and environmentally friendly products / are formulated without animal testing.

This cosmetic collection, which, has been dermatologically tested, is famous for its soft, natural colours & textures which are easily adapted from day to evening wear.

9

© LCCI 1994

← All these notes are to be inserted as instructed on the previous page, but do not type the numbers.

Notes

1 This original double spaced draft has been amended by your employer. After checking your instructions, read through the content carefully.

2 You will need to incorporate information from the separate page into the appropriate places on this draft.

3 Display the assignment so that the information on this conference handout will be easy for delegates to refer to.

Unit **6**

Full examination practice

I hope that you now have a thorough understanding of the expectations of the Manuscript Transcription examination and are feeling confident that you can attempt the examination successfully.

Now it is time to put all the theory into practice as you attempt the full examination papers from the June 1995 SSC and PSC examinations.

Treat each of these papers as a real examination, remembering the importance of the 15 minutes' reading time. For final guidance, here are two checklists for you to consider – the first listing questions which you should ask yourself after the 15 minutes' reading time before beginning transcription; the second listing questions which you should ask yourself after completing all the assignments before handing your completed work to your tutor for marking.

Good luck with your examinations!

Questions to ask yourself *before* transcribing the assignments

Have I . . .

1   read the Instruction Sheet carefully and

● highlighted the way the employer wishes his/her name to be displayed on letters?
● made a note of the reference to be used in all assignments?
● become familiar with any special instructions provided, and names and addresses needed during transcription?

2   read through the entire paper and become familiar with the integrated theme connecting the assignments?

3   made a note at the head of each assignment regarding:

● the type of paper to use when transcribing the document?
● any special reminders such as names/titles for memos, etc?

4 studied each assignment carefully and made adequate preparations to help when transcribing, such as:

- highlighted special instructions regarding display, enumeration, spacing, headings etc?
- checked all correction signs, amendments and insertions to ensure correct interpretation?
- crossed out instructions like 'Ask him . . . '? and noted appropriate rephrasing?
- changed pronouns to 'she' and 'you' as necessary?
- written out appropriate abbreviations in full?
- noted where new paragraphs should begin?
- noted subject heading to be used where appropriate?
- noted 'Enc' at the foot where appropriate?
- noted the reference and date on each assignment as a reminder?
- made any necessary calculations?

Questions to ask yourself *after* transcribing all the assignments

Have I . . .

1 followed all the employer's instructions?

2 interpreted the employer's requirements correctly?

3 transcribed an accurate interpretation of the employer's meaning?

4 used appropriate paper for each assignment?

5 included all relevant details, in particular:

- names/designations on memos?
- subject headings on memos?
- inside address details on letters?
- salutation/complimentary close on letters?
- reference and date on all assignments?
- continuation sheet headings where necessary?
- 'Enc' where appropriate?

6 checked through each assignment to ensure complete sense?

7 used appropriate display, considering the purpose of each document?

8 ensured consistency within each assignment and throughout the entire examination?

9 proofread each assignment carefully and corrected any errors?

10 ensured that all documents are mailable?

JUNE SERIES 1995

SECRETARIAL STUDIES CERTIFICATE EXAMINATION

COMMUNICATION - TRANSCRIPTION - MANUSCRIPT

WEDNESDAY 7 JUNE 1995 – 1400 to 1615

———————

Instructions to Candidates

*(a)   The time allowed for this examination is **2** hours **15** minutes.*

*(b)   Candidates must be allowed **15** minutes to study these instructions and the examination paper before commencing the transcription.*

(c)   Candidates must read the examination paper carefully to find the necessary information to complete the assignments.

*(d)   The time allowed for transcription is **2** hours.*

INFORMATION FOR CANDIDATES

The candidate works for Jonathan Stewart, Editor of IN TUNE Music Magazine owned by Comlon International plc. The Company produces records, cassettes and CDs. IN TUNE is a magazine for classical music lovers.

Mr Stewart likes his letters to be completed in the following way

JONATHAN STEWART
Editor, IN TUNE Music Magazine

You will need the following information

Jane Clark
Competitions Editor

Leslie Martin
21 Heathfield Avenue
London
W13 7BG

Paul Eversham

Alexander French

Robert Wilson
Glebe Cottage
Campden
TK15 7LW

Pamela Shaw
29 Mill Lane
Wincot
CM2 3MD

Peter Sampson

Julia Gregg
Subscriptions Department

Brian Forman
Features Department

CONSISTENT USE OF ANY STYLE OF PUNCTUATION AND LAYOUT IS ACCEPTABLE

NOTES

(a) Envelopes are **NOT** required.

(b) Candidates must use Originator/Typist reference initials on each piece of work.

(c) Each piece of work must be dated with the date of the examination unless otherwise instructed.

(d) Arrange papers in order of dictation in the bag-envelope provided.

(e) Unused examination material should **not** be returned.

(f) The use of standard English dictionaries and cordless non-programmable calculators is permitted. Candidates whose first language is not English may use a bilingual dictionary.

Further instructions are given on each assignment.

MESSAGE TO SECRETARY: Please type these tasks for me as I shall be out of the office all day.

Memo to Competitions Editor — urgent

CD Competition Result

This is a reminder that the deadline for publication in the August edition of

Caps In Tune is Friday 30 June. As discussed by telephone I must have full details of the winners of your June competition

NP as soon as possible. [I am holding a page to feature the results of this competition which I thought was particularly interesting. This affects the index on page 1 of the magazine

NP + the layout of the cover. [If you cannot supply names, addresses or possibly photographs, in time, please let me have some material to maintain interest; a paragraph of 50-100 words (including the answers to the questions) would be sufficient.

NP [Readers are always very interested in the results of competitions. We must try to

NP publish results as promised. [Please telephone me immediately ~~on~~ after your return from the Truro Festival.

Unit 6 Full examination practice

Assignment 2

Write a letter to Mr L Martin —
you have his address. Head it MUSIC
IN ART. Thank him for his letter of
appreciation about the article published in the March issue
Caps of _In Tune_ — always pleased to receive
comments on contributions.
Say we hope to publish a series on
Caps _Poetry in Music_ beginning September —
articles in the form of discussions
between our well-known classical
music writer Brian Forman & modern
poets such as Paul Eversham &
Alexander French. ＊Hope he'll
like the articles — comments please.

Add to end of para 2

＊ So much of the classical music
repertory is based on, or inspired
by, poetry. Equally fascinating are
the poets whose work is lost to us
except for fragments transformed
into powerful songs.

147

Retype in 1½ line spacing. Omit material between square brackets [ ]

Assignment 3

COMPOSER OF THE MONTH

EDWARD ELGAR 1857-1934
BORN BROADHEATH, WORCESTERSHIRE, 2 JUNE 1857
DIED WORCESTER, 23 FEBRUARY 1934

Sixty years after Elgar's death [the flood of fresh material rises all the time.] Surely more is now known about Elgar than ever before. Elgar's birthplace is [the subject of national concern] so many pilgrims visit the little cottage at Broadheath [village near Worcester] that it is in danger of becoming damaged.

[And yet ... Sometimes it seems that] the more *that* is known *about him* the more enigmatic he becomes. He *Elgar* rose from humble obscurity to the highest honours, unlike, say, Parry or Vaughan Williams who were born with social advantages. Neither his life nor his music is simple. There are layers of meaning, contradictions, ambiguities. Elgar and his music grew and changed.

Some The little group of his cronies are now familiar worldwide through the Enigma Variations but it is the quality of the music, the actual notes and invention, that makes them so. In the end what matters is not just the experience of the man but the leap of his imagination and that, no one can explain.

Elgar bought his first bicycle in 1900. [He called it Mr Phoebus after the Roman god of music and nature] And after mornings spent slaving over the manuscript paper in his study Elgar would cycle for up to 50 miles *through* down the Malvern lanes to compose. It has been suggested that the regular rhythm of walking and cycling provided Elgar with an in-built metronome for his invention *Compositions.*

Elgar virtually stopped composing in the years in which he took to the motor car but these were also the years following the death of his wife Alice. The flow of *his* great works dried up while Elgar lived in London. It was not until he discovered a pied-a-terre in deepest Sussex that he wrote the music of three chamber pieces and his final masterpiece, the Cello Concerto.

He told his friends he had to go down to Longdon Marsh to think through difficult passages in THE APOSTLES.

Assignment 4

Letter to Robert Wilson

Dear Robert

HAYDN SCOOP OF THE CENTURY

Thank you for your article exploring
the development of the ⟨piano⟩ ~~Concertos~~ [Haydn sonatas]
[recent] & the importance of the ⟨discovery⟩ in
Germany of manuscript copies of 6
lost sonatas. ←

NP ⌈Please telephone me to make an
appointment to meet to discuss

Trs   ✗ 2. possible illustrations;   ↰
        ✗ 1 additional historical background;
        3 future concerts & recitals to which
        the article could be linked.

NP ⌈I should like to use this material in a
future edition of the magazine — the sooner
the better because of its topicality. I
think this could be expanded to a full
page article.

149

Letter to Mrs P Shaw about re-issues.
Acknowledge her letter about recently
re-issued recordings. Make the following
points.

1 She's a new subscriber so will
have missed the series about this
published last year.

2 The Tchaikovsky Piano Concerto No.1
& the Violin Concerto in D were
featured in January 1994.

3 Insert the summary of Peter Sampson's
review I have attached. (Peter
is an expert in 19th century music)

4 Past editions of the magazine can
be obtained from Subscriptions Depart.
or telephone Julia Gregg extension 250.

TCHAIKOVSKY

Piano Concerto No 1 in B Flat minor
Violin Concerto in D

Comlon label: Emma Hinds (piano); Foo Tin (violin); Ultra Symphonia conducted
by Alan Rand.

These concertos are two of the most popular in the repertoire. Both soloists
capture the power and subtlety of the composer: they interpret well, supported
by the orchestra and controlled by the conductor.

Recommended as the CD BUY OF THE MONTH.

Memo to Brian Forman

COMPOSER OF THE MONTH

Thank you for your article
about Elgar,↓ I am sorry
I have had to edit it rather
severely to fit into the allotted
space. (Copy of which I return.)

Please telephone me if you
wish to discuss my amendments.

JUNE SERIES 1995

PRIVATE SECRETARY'S CERTIFICATE EXAMINATION

COMMUNICATION - TRANSCRIPTION - MANUSCRIPT - PAPER A

WEDNESDAY 14 JUNE 1995 – 1400 to 1615

Instructions to Candidates

(a)   *The time allowed for this examination is **2** hours **15** minutes.*

(b)   *Candidates must be allowed **15** minutes to study these instructions and the examination paper before commencing the transcription.*

(c)   *Candidates must read the examination paper carefully to find the necessary information to complete the assignments.*

(d)   *The time allowed for transcription is **2** hours.*

INFORMATION FOR CANDIDATES

The candidate works for Elizabeth Sutton, Manager, Public Relations, Comlon International plc. The Company produces health foods and soft drinks. Mrs Sutton and her colleague, Ms Angela Sanders, Manager, Advertising, are liaising to complete arrangements for a Press Conference to be held on 18 July to introduce a new fruit drink, POMALLA.

Mrs Sutton likes her letters to be completed in the following way

ELIZABETH SUTTON (Mrs)
Manager, Public Relations

You will need the following information

David Whitmore   Howard Mason
2 Well Close   Managing Director
Babbington
TA15 7BJ

CONSISTENT USE OF ANY STYLE OF PUNCTUATION AND LAYOUT IS ACCEPTABLE

NOTES

(a) Envelopes are **NOT** required.

(b) Candidates must use Originator/Typist reference initials on each piece of work.

(c) Each piece of work must be dated with the date of the examination unless otherwise instructed.

(d) Arrange papers in order of dictation in the bag-envelope provided.

(e) Unused examination material should **not** be returned.

(f) The use of standard English dictionaries and cordless non-programmable calculators is permitted. Candidates whose first language is not English may use a bilingual dictionary.

Further instructions are given on each assignment.

2

Write to David Whitmore about the Conference

Dear David I am glad that you will be able
to attend our POMALLA Press Conference / To introduce POMALLA
on Tuesday 18 July. I am grateful to you for
NP being prepared to face interviews and sign
autographs if required. [Arrangements have been
made to hold the launch of this new product
in the Conference Centre / I enclose a provisional
(at Coulon House.)
NP timetable, still to be confirmed by our Managing
discussed Director who is abroad at present. [As we
0930. Your ⅕ minute talk about the benefits of health
drinks should ~~commence~~ start about 1045.

NP [The Directors & Managers of Coulon ----. Me
4/c invite you to lunch in the ORTANIQUE ROOM
at 1300 and wish you every success for your
participation in the World Transplant Games
in Australia.

NP ([I have asked for questions in writing for the
Panel session. I shall let you have details
nearer the time.)

Assignment 2

(POMALLA) LAUNCH OF ←

PRESS CONFERENCE 18 JULY 1995

in the Conference Centre, Cowlon House

PROVISIONAL PROGRAMME ←

u/s or
emboldew   0930   Photo call
o/o   Press to meet and photograph David Whitmore with advertising
                        display, and sample fruit juices.

            1030   Journalists assemble for Press Conference

            1045   Managing Director introduces
                                                        briefly
                            1   David Whitmore to talk /about health drinks
                            2   Advertising Manager to give details of the new product

u/s or
bold   1115   Question Time
                        Panel: Managing Director, Advertising Manager, David Whitmore

            1145   Members of the Panel available for individual interviews

            1200   Bar opens
                        Invited members of the Press to pre-lunch drinks followed by a
                        buffet lunch / in the Mandarin Room.
                        Managing Director, David Whitmore and selected guests to drinks
                        in Clementines and lunch / in the Ortanique Room.

NP   Advert. Dept. to set up display during Monday
17 July o to be responsible for seating arrangements,
                (including folders and samples)
advertising material /and all audio/visual
equipment. [Public Relations Dept. will be
responsible for sending invitations, producing a
Press Release and organising refreshments and
lunches.
Both departments will liaise with the Chief
Security Officer to ensure maximum security.

A memo please from me to the Managing
Director about the Conference.

Tell him arrangements are almost complete.

I : enclose draft Press Release and
provisional programme

shall be pleased to make amendments
if we can discuss when he returns
from Europe next week

have contacted David Whitmore & am
sure his presence will interest Press.
am liaising closely with Advert. Dept.
& Security ↗

am very pleased he will be able to attend.

Say we have been working towards this for a
long time & wish to ensure a successful
launch.

Assignment 4

Please draft an invitation to the
Press Conference for members of the
Press who will be invited to pre-lunch
drinks and Buffet in the Mandarin
Room. You have all the details.
RSVP <u>before 10 July</u> to me.
When I have approved your draft
we can ask Print Dept. to print
as invitation card.

Remember to leave a space for me to
fill in the name of the person I want
to invite and type PRESS in the top right
corner.

DRAFT ~~(PLEASE TYPE ON HEADED PAPER)~~

PRESS RELEASE   FOR 18 JULY 1995

POMALLA FRUIT JUICE

NP A Press Conference will be held in the Conference Centre, Comlon House on Tuesday 18 July 1995 to introduce POMALLA, [This latest addition to the Comlon range of fruit juices blends seven delicious fruit flavours into one tangy refreshing drink. *run on*

u/c ~~It is~~ low in calories and rich in vitamins ~~and~~ combines all the *health-giving POMALLA* virtues
u/c of the juices of pineapples, oranges, mandarins, apricots, lemons, limes
u/c and apples.

The Comlon
refined over many years g ~~Our~~ formula combined with special methods of juice extraction and preservation has resulted in a unique drink which has been tasted and approved by the Comlon Athlete of the Year, David Whitmore.

NP David ~~had~~ achieved many honours in international athletics before ill-health forced him to abandon his successful career. [David says: When I had to change my life-style I found that Comlon fruit juices provided the healthy drinks I needed. *I shall find POMALLA particularly refr in the high temperatures in Australia where I shall be competing*
NP POMALLA contains no artificial flavourings, colours or sweeteners. ~~It can be~~ Served *chilled* straight from the bottle or mixed with a favourite still
4c or sparkling mineral water, *POMALLA provides delicious and*

healthy refreshment.

NP [NUTRITION INFORMATION per 100 ml

Energy	1.74 Kj/41 Kcal
Protein	0.1 g
Carbohydrate	9.8 g
Fat	Trace
Vitamin C	not less than 24 mg

POMALLA will be sold in half-litre and one-litre bottles for retail outlets and half-gallon containers for catering establishments. *For the takeaway trade POMALLA will be available in quarter-litre bottles.*

At the age of 35 he was given a heart transplant and within 18 months he was running, jumping o swimming in the World Transplant Games in Vancouver, Canada, where he won 2 gold medals and a silver medal. Comlon is proud to be associated with this dedicated athlete who was named Comlon Athlete of the Year in 1994. The Company will sponsor David's entry into the next series of the Games.

Assignment 6

Please answer this letter using the notes given below.

32 Maple Drive
Littlehampton
Sussex
BN16 7EK

1 June 1995

Mrs E Sutton
Public Relations Manager
Comlon International plc
Comlon House
West Street
LONDON   SW1Y 2AR

Dear Mrs Sutton

Recently I read an article in a magazine about healthy drinking. The
writer praised a Comlon product called, I think, Pamola or Pomala which
contains the juices of several different fruits. It sounded delicious
and was said to contain no artificial flavouring, colouring or
sweeteners.

I have enquired at all my local stores and supermarkets but none has
this drink on its shelves. I am sure this was mentioned as a Comlon
product because I have always purchased Comlon health foods and I have
been very satisfied with them.

As your name was given on a carton of orange juice I purchased last week
I decided to write to you. Please let me know if Comlon sells a multi-
juice fruit drink and where I can obtain it.

Yours sincerely

Pauline Winter (MRS)

Acknowledge; interested she had read the article in
THE WAY TO HEALTH commending POMALLA. Give details
of the product using paras 2 and 6 of the Press Release.
Say that POMALLA will be launched on 18 July followed
by special displays in foodstores and supermarkets
country-wide. Enclose voucher to entitle her to a free
one-litre bottle from any store displaying Comlon
Health Foods Sign. Hope she enjoys it & continues to
buy Comlon health foods.

LCCI CET 1995

159

LC
CI

LONDON
CHAMBER
of
COMMERCE &
INDUSTRY
COMMERCIAL
EDUCATION
TRUST
**EXAMINATIONS
BOARD**

JUNE SERIES 1995

PRIVATE SECRETARY'S CERTIFICATE EXAMINATION

COMMUNICATION - TRANSCRIPTION - MANUSCRIPT - PAPER B

WEDNESDAY 14 JUNE 1995 – 1400 to 1615

Instructions to Candidates

*(a)   The time allowed for this examination is **2** hours **15** minutes.*

*(b)   Candidates must be allowed **15** minutes to study these instructions and the examination paper before commencing the transcription.*

(c)   Candidates must read the examination paper carefully to find the necessary information to complete the assignments.

*(d)   The time allowed for transcription is **2** hours.*

INFORMATION FOR CANDIDATES

The candidate works for Angela Sanders, Manager, Advertising, Comlon International plc. The Company produces fruit drinks and health foods and will introduce a new fruit drink, POMALLA, at a Press Conference to be held in the Conference Centre, Comlon House, on Tuesday 18 July 1995. Ms Sanders and Mrs Sutton are liaising about the arrangements for the launch.

Ms Sanders likes her letters to be completed in the following way

ANGELA SANDERS
Manager, Advertising

You will need the following information

David Whitmore
2 Well Close
Babbington
TA15 7BJ

Elizabeth Sutton
Manager, Public Relations

Hillview Studios
Long Avenue
Bushey
Herts
WD3 4NB

CONSISTENT USE OF ANY STYLE OF PUNCTUATION AND LAYOUT IS ACCEPTABLE

NOTES

(a) Envelopes are **NOT** required.

(b) Candidates must use Originator/Typist reference initials on each piece of work.

(c) Each piece of work must be dated with the date of the examination unless otherwise instructed.

(d) Arrange papers in order of dictation in the bag-envelope provided.

(e) Unused examination material should **not** be returned.

(f) The use of standard English dictionaries and cordless non-programmable calculators is permitted. Candidates whose first language is not English may use a bilingual dictionary.

Further instructions are given on each assignment.

2

Send a letter to David Whitmore about his television advertising contract.

Dear David, I am sorry I was not in the office when you telephoned yesterday. I confirm that the terms of your television advertising contract have been agreed

NP [Your first assignment will be on Thursday 20 July at 1030 to make a video advert. for Comlon fruit juices. I enclose a draft script. The video will be made at ------ and (please fill in address of the studios) will be produced by Robert Mason. I enclose a map to help you to find the studios. I can arrange transport for you if required.

                  that
NP [I suggest/we meet here some time during the next two weeks so that we can discuss the script & other details. Please telephone
                          agree
my secretary to ~~suggest~~ a convenient date and time.

(and that you will receive your contract from our Legal Department within the next few days.)

Assignment 2

ADVERTCO Plc

invites

<u>M̲s̲ A̲N̲G̲E̲L̲A̲ S̲A̲N̲D̲E̲R̲S̲ ̲a̲n̲d̲ P̲A̲R̲T̲N̲E̲R̲</u>

to the

Inaugural Meeting of the Advertising Associates of London

at

ADVER HOUSE GUILD LANE LONDON E10 2AF

Tuesday 8 August 1995

1930 for 2000

Buffet Supper

RSVP Roslyn Finlay
Adver House
Room 206   Telephone 0171-249 9989

Please acknowledge this with a personal letter
to Roslyn. Regret I cannot attend as I
shall be in Italy. Send her association
my best wishes for the future. If she
wishes to invite a rep. from this company
I can recommend my colleague, Mrs Elizabeth
Sutton, manager, Public Relations. I have
contacted her and she would be willing to
attend, if Roslyn likes to send her an
official invitation.

Press Conference - Pomalla launch - 18 July.

Advert. Dept to be responsible for

1. Advertising display - set up 17 July. -
Supply display boards, advert. material
including visual aids eg videos, films, tapes.
Provide & check necessary equipment eg screens,
video/film projectors & cassette player

2. Seating - arrange theatre style seating
for approx. 100 guests

3. Samples - ensure sufficient quantity of
Pomalla in ¼ - litre bottles for sample to
be given to all who attend - to be
informed of final number of acceptances
by 1200 17 July.

These are my notes of my telephone conversation
with Elizabeth Sutton. Send her a memo thanking
her for making the initial arrangements for the
conference and confirm our responsibilities. I
understand Public Relations will deal with invitations,
preparing a Press Release and all arrangements for
refreshments and lunches. Staffing to be covered
by both departments. Suggest we meet one day
next week to discuss final details.

Assignment 4

Please type on headed paper

COMLON FRESHLY SQUEEZED JUICE — HEALTHY AND NATURAL

O R A N G E

¶ [~~Like all fresh Comlon products Comlon orange juice is just 100 per cent natural juice and does not contain any preservatives, concentrates or additives~~.] The "Golden Apple" of Greek mythology, the orange is probably the most popular of the citrus family. It was first cultivated by the Chinese as early as 2000 BC but it is only in this century that it has been valued ∧ *has a rich source of vitamin C.*

O R T A N I Q U E

l/c Trs ∧ *The* ∧ *The* Ortanique is a/ *hybrid* fruit developed in Jamaica by c~~r~~ossing species of orange and tangerine. / I~~ts~~ juice has a delicately sweet and refreshing flavour. *of this exotic fruit*

C L E M E N T I N E

The clementine is a variety of mandarin∧ *orange* which originated in East Asia. ∧ *in 1902* The fruit is a cross between several species discovered by accident / in the garden of Father Pierre Clement in Algeria∧ *hence the name.* ∧ Clementine juice has a sweet flavour and a delicate aroma.

P I N K   O R A N G E

¶ Most varieties of pink orange originated in the Mediterranean area. *with pink flesh* Some of the islands such as Sicily and Malta have grown ~~pink~~ oranges∧ for centuries. The colour of these oranges varies but their juice has a distinctive fragrance and refreshing taste.

S W E E T   G R A P E F R U I T

The grapefruit/ *is so called because it* grows in clusters like grapes. ~~Descended from~~/ *It is a descendant of* a large citrus fruit called Shaddock introduced in the 17th Century by Captain Shaddock. The modern grapefruit has become popular because it is thought to speed up metabolism and aid slimming. The juices of the pink-fleshed varieties of the fruit make a delicious rose-coloured drink.

¶/c ALL COMLON PRODUCTS CONTAIN 100 per cent natural juice — no preservatives, concentrates or additives.

Please type as amended with abbreviations in full

Assignment 5

PUBLICITY MATERIAL FOR PRESS CONFERENCE FOLDER 18 JULY

COMLON FRESHLY SQUEEZED FRUIT JUICES

For Comlon quality and freshness come first - our customers will vouch for that.

We at Comlon are continually expanding our range of citrus fruit juices and more ~~fruit and vegetable products~~ *varieties* are to be launched soon.

Our tight quality control system ensures consistent flavour and goodness throughout the year.

To meet the expectations of the health-conscious consumer all our fresh products are prepared daily without the use of additives, preservatives or heat treatment.

Comlon products can be found on the shelves of many supermarkets and appear on the stocklists of numerous hotels, airlines and catering establishments.

NP [Some of the fruits we use are seasonal. ~~Details~~ Periods of availability are shown below.

FRESHLY SQUEEZED FRUIT JUICES

PRODUCT	AVAILABILITY
ORANGE	ALL YEAR
SWEET GRAPEFRUIT	ALL YEAR
Caps Pink Orange	FEB. - MAY
ORTANIQUE	JAN - APRIL
CLEMENTINE	NOV - Feb Caps
LEMON & LIME	ALL YEAR

NP [All freshly squeezed fruit juices have a shelf life of 8 days from the date on the packaging. Once the package has been opened the juice should be kept in a refrigerator and consumed within 3 days.

↳(chilled)

COMLON FRUIT JUICE DRINKS — NATURALLY FRESH AND HEALTHY

Send a memo to all senior staff to inform
them that the next meeting of the department
will be Wed. 21 June, 1400 Room A Conference
Centre.

Add an Agenda — usual routine items.

Special matters for discussion are

Press Conference for Pomalla launch
Arrangements for displays; advert. material;
seating; equipment; supply of samples.
Liaison with Public Relations Dept.

Conference staffing.

Television advertising by David Whitmore

Next meeting will be Wed. 19 July — same time.

Suggested answers and check copies

Unit I

```
M E M O R A N D U M

To     Pamela Tyler, Secretarial Services Supervisor

From   Eileen Forrest, General Manager

Ref    EF/ST

Date   20 April 1994 (accept any appropriate date)


NEW TELEPHONE EXCHANGE

It has been decided to install a new telephone exchange so
that communication links with branches is improved.

It is proposed to employ 2 operators on a rota system
covering the hours from 0800 to 1800.  Full training will,
of course, be provided.

Could you please recommend 3 or 4 candidates from your
department who would be willing to train as operators of the
new exchange.

Please let me have their names before 5 March.

If you have any queries please let me know.
```

Unit 3

```
M E M O R A N D U M

To    Maureen Taylor, Assistant Company Secretary

From  Jane Wittington, Editor, Sweet News

Ref   JW/ST

Date  9 December 1992


THE HISTORY OF CHOCOLATE

Thank you for your interesting contribution for Sweet News
on the history of chocolate.  I should like to use it for our
special Centenary edition.

I have made some amendments to your work.  A copy is
enclosed.  Would you have lunch with me next week so that we
can discuss this?  I am free on 16 or 17 December but if you
prefer we can leave it until after Christmas, as we shall not
print the Centenary edition until June.

Please let my secretary know which dates are convenient for
you.



Enc
```

Unit 3

Comlon International plc

Comlon House West Street London SW1Y 2AR

tel: 0181 302 0261
telex: Comlond 888941   telemessages: Comlond London SW1   fax: 0181 302 4169

PT/ST

4 June 1995

Mrs Loretta Jones
Training and Development Manager
GMB Engineering plc
Units 12-16
23 Tower Industrial Estate
NOTTINGHAM
NG2 3JT

Dear Mrs Jones

Thank you for your letter of 1 June. I am very happy to
accept your invitation to make a presentation at your seminar
on the topic of Human Relationships at Work. The date and
time you mentioned will be quite convenient for me.

I have a 20 minute film which I am sure delegates would find
interesting, so I hope it will be possible to make a projector
available. A flip chart would also be useful.

As I am not familiar with the Nottingham area, I would
appreciate it if you could let me have a map showing
directions to the venue.

I look forward to hearing further from you soon.

Yours sincerely

PATRICK THOMPSON
Operations Director
Comlon Hotels

Unit 3

INTRODUCTION TO POLESDEN LACEY by S J Shepherd

The house is beautifully situated on high ground, with a fine view from the south terrace across the park-like landscape to the Ranmore woods on the far side of the valley. Beyond the woods lies Ranmore Common. Above Burford Bridge to the east are the steep slopes of Box Hill.

The present mansion was begun in 1824 by Joseph Bonsor to the designs of Thomas Cubitt. It is a pleasant low building of two storeys, surrounding an open central courtyard, with roughcast and yellow washed walls. Though the interior of the house has been entirely reconstructed since it was built, the exterior has been less altered and preserves something of its Regency Villa style. The south front with its Ionic colonnade is original but an eastward extension has been added to provide a suite of private rooms.

The east front has undergone the greatest changes. A cupola was added and, at the entrance Joseph Bonsor's Doric portico was taken down and the columns re-erected in the form of a screen at the far end of the Long Walk. The visitor enters through a new entrance, built for Sir Clinton Dawkins. The house was damaged by fire in 1960 but re-opened in 1962 after careful restoration.

PW/ST
1 December 1993

Unit 3

```
RECOMMENDED LOW PRICE HOTELS

ITALY


ROME

Hotel Windsor, Via Magna Grecia
Central, near St John's in Laterano
56 rooms all with bath/shower, air conditioning, telephone,
radio, colour TV.  Panoramic views of city.

MILAN

Hotel Irma, Via Lepetit
Central, near Duomo
52 rooms all with private facilities, air conditioning,
telephone, radio/TV.  Some rooms have balconies.


SWITZERLAND

GENEVA

Hotel Mont Blanc, Avenue de Frontenex
Quiet position, 5 minutes from lake and city centre
49 rooms, all with usual facilities; some with balcony.

LAUSANNE

Hotel Beau Rivage, Avenue de Cour
Overlooking Lake Geneva
50 rooms with usual facilities and mini-bar.  Completely
renovated 1990.  Some rooms with balconies and superb views
of the lake.  (Note: Roadside rooms can be noisy)


GERMANY

MUNICH

Hotel Park, Schillerstrasse
Central, near station
50 rooms all with bath, telephone, TV and mini-bar.
Comfortable but could be noisy.  Recommended for night stops
only.


Rates at all these hotels come within our 'C' band and
charges include continental breakfast.




GB/ST
8 December 1993
```

Unit 3

D I A M O N D   J U B I L E E

C O M P E T I T I O N

Can YOU suggest a name for
the Company's new drinking chocolate?

The Advertising Executive Committee
is organising an interdepartmental competition
to find a descriptive name which will be
marketable and easy to advertise

Special features of the new drinking chocolate are

***

QUICK AND EASY TO MAKE

HEATS IN ONE MINUTE IN A MICROWAVE - NO MESS, NO FUSS

MADE WITH SEMI-SKIMMED MILK - IDEAL FOR WEIGHT WATCHERS

FULL OF THAT SPECIAL COMLON TASTE

***

Ideas should be submitted
only on the official entry form
obtainable from

Customer Relations Manager's Secretary

MJ/ST
2 December 1992

Unit 3.1

M E M O R A N D U M

To   David Simmons, Chief Editor

From   Paul Winter, Editor, Historic Houses

Ref   PW/ST

Date   1 December 1993

HISTORIC HOUSES - NEW PUBLICATIONS

As Volume 2 of Historic Houses is nearly complete, I should like to discuss with you the possibility of publishing a smaller volume (or separate books) about some of the smaller but very interesting properties for which there was no room in our present publication.

I would like to suggest separate low cost volumes for different areas, eg Wales, Scotland, South West England and so on.

I enclose descriptions of the houses in Wales which I have already researched, also a list of others which I think are worth considering.

I will telephone you when you return from New York to find out if you approve so that I can start contacting authors.

Encs

Unit 3.2

Comlon International plc

Comlon House West Street London SW1Y 2AR

tel: 0181 302 0261
telex: Comlond 888941 telemessages: Comlond London SW1 fax: 0181 302 4169

JW/ST

9 December 1992

Mr J S Short
General Manager
The Westin Hotel
Cranbrook Road
Slough
Berks
SL2 3YB

Dear Mr Short

CONFERENCE FACILITIES RESERVATION - PRIZE AWARDS

Thank you for your letter of 8 December.

I confirm the reservation of the Princess Suite for
Wednesday 17 February 1993 and appreciate your kind offer of
a 25% discount. In the conference room we shall require the
use of a VHS video cassette player, a slide carousel and a
large screen.

Two double rooms will also be required for the night of
16 February.

Mr Martin Gardner, our Press Officer, and I would like to
see the facilities and discuss menus at 1000 on 7 January if
this is convenient. Please telephone my secretary to confirm
this appointment or to make alternative arrangements.

Yours sincerely

JANE WITTINGTON (Miss)
Editor, Sweet News

Unit 3.3

NEW UK FRANCHISES SPECIALISING IN FAST FOOD

SUGGESTIONS FOR PUBLICITY AND PROMOTIONS
AIMED AT YOUNG PEOPLE (for discussion)

1   PUBLICITY - advertising in

    1.1   local newspapers

    1.2   local radio

    1.3   national TV at children's viewing time

2   PROMOTIONS

    2.1   Competitions eg quizzes, puzzles, painting and
        drawing (with prizes of free meal vouchers to be
        spent at new fast food outlets)

    2.2   Children's special occasion functions eg birthday
        parties, end-of-term celebrations

    2.3   Giveaways eg special occasion favours, balloons,
        paper hats (all with a fish motif - see below)

    2.4   The creation of a comic character designed to
        appeal to children. (I am sure one of our artists
        could create a cartoon fish which could be
        incorporated in the franchise logo design.)

    2.5   The use of this cartoon character in animated
        advertisements

    2.6   Lucky Draws

    2.7   Special discount offers

    2.8   Special children's menus.

JH/ST
16 June 1993

Unit 3.4

M E M O R A N D U M

To   Mark McNally, Conferences Manager
      (Display and Exhibits)

From Anne Richards, Conferences Manager (Administration)

Ref   AR/ST

Date 9 June 1993

MONTHLY PLANNING MEETING

The next monthly Planning Meeting will be held in my office
at 1000 on Monday 14 June.

The main item for discussion will be the conference and
exhibition for manufacturers and distributors of self-
assembly furniture to be held in Birmingham next May.
Therefore, please come prepared to report on progress to
date in your areas.

A G E N D A

1 Minutes of last meeting

2 Matters arising

3 Arrangements for Birmingham Conference 10-13 May 1994

   3.1 Administration (Anne Richards to report)
   3.2 Display and Exhibits (Mark McNally and
        Sarah Fletcher)
   3.3 Programme (Dominic Mason)
   3.4 Support Systems (Jill Cartwright)

4 New Edinburgh Conference Centre
   (Anne Richards to report developments)

5 Any Other Business

6 Date and time of next meeting
   (1000, Monday 19 July 1993)

Copies to: Jill Cartwright, Support Systems Organiser
            Sarah Fletcher, Deputy Conference Manager
            Dominic Mason, Programme Organiser

Unit 5

PSC December 1994 Examiner's Report

GENERAL COMMENTS

A few candidates submitted scripts of a very good standard and were awarded high distinction marks; the majority passed but failed to attain the best marks of which they were capable because of carelessness and disregard to instructions. The failures were generally attributable to poor proofreading.

Some points of display should be noted:

1   Letterhead paper should not be used for memos. Memo paper is not provided so that candidates can use their own format using plain bond.

2   There is confusion and inconsistency in the use of the dash and hyphen. There should be a space before and after the symbol when used as a dash. The hyphen usually joins 2 parts of a word and should not be spaced.

3   An unnecessarily large space is often left <u>before</u> the complimentary close. A double line space after the last paragraph is sufficient. Students who did this frequently left insufficient space for the signature which should be at least 4 spaces before the name and designation.

4   Candidates should remember that corrections show if not typed over; too many typists type into the right-hand margin then paint out or lift off the word leaving an unsightly correction in the margin.

ASSIGNMENT 1

Many candidates need more practice in composition from notes. These should be expanded and correctly punctuated with the pronouns changed where necessary. Although the two main items for this memo were numbered in the notes because they were separate subjects, few candidates typed them in this way. Run together as one paragraph it gave the impression that the follow-up courses were for voice-activated PCs. That this was not so should have been obvious from the programme (Assignment 2). Candidates should read the whole paper through carefully in the 15 minutes allowed before the commencement of the examination, noting the relationship of one assignment to another so that each is not treated as an isolated task.

ASSIGNMENT 2

In spite of the instruction to type the aim of the course, duration and dates on separate lines, some candidates produced elaborate tabular programmes. When displaying this type of material the convenience of the reader should be considered. In this case the course and its aim would probably be the information sought first and would need to be emphasised by underscore, capitals or emboldening, followed by the duration, times, dates. Some were not even consistent, starting each course with a different piece of information. The date and reference must be typed at the bottom of plain paper.

Unit 5
PSC December 1994 Examiner's Report

ASSIGNMENT 3

This assignment caused few problems except the usual careless proofreading. The roller-ball mouse appeared in several disguises.

ASSIGNMENT 4

This was a straightforward assignment for which candidates created their own difficulties; another instance of insufficient use of the preparation time. In spite of the clear salutation "Dear Paul" many candidates began their letter "Dear Mr Chan" or, occasionally, "Dear Sir". Two candidates typed the whole of the article; some ignored the instruction to type only the words between the square brackets and included the whole of the heading, while others overlooked paragraph 1 and/or paragraph 6 altogether. This assignment and assignment 5 gave plenty of scope for typographical errors. It is obvious that candidates work too quickly knowing that they have easy correcting devices but then fail to notice their errors and correct them. Although a continuation page was not necessary some candidates (probably those who typed too much of the article) took a second page. Continuation pages, if required, should be typed on plain, not letterhead, paper.

ASSIGNMENT 5

Sadly many typographical errors were made in the typescript for which there was no excuse. The only manuscript word which appeared to give trouble was "distinctly" appearing as "districtly" or "distinctively". "She spooked districtly" was probably the weirdest transcription! Occasionally paragraphs were omitted or misplaced but uncorrected errors, more than 12 in some cases, caused several candidates to fail this assignment.

ASSIGNMENT 6

This, like Assignment 1, produced some badly worded letters. Carelessness or undue haste caused some candidates to address the letter to M̲r̲ Watson or even Mr Clare; many forgot to address the letter c/o Monsieur Jean Bouchon, Directeur; some c̲o̲m̲m̲a̲n̲d̲e̲d̲ her to stay in France. Those who had read the paper thoroughly and related the tasks pointed out that the a̲d̲v̲a̲n̲c̲e̲d̲ courses commenced on 18 March (not all courses).

Overseas candidates particularly have problems with the tenses of verbs and should give special attention to phrases which frequently occur in letters eg "I enclose", "I am enclosing" but "a copy is enclosed". Some are using old-fashioned language eg "Please be informed". Why not simply give the information? "Thank you" is often offered as an unnecessary final paragraph. Often the wrong verb followed a plural noun eg "These courses i̲s̲ useful" instead of "are". Other common errors were "We plan to introduced"; "If you telephones". "A" and "the" were often omitted.

Unit 5
PSC December 1994 Check Copies

M E M O R A N D U M

To   Audrey James, Divisional Manager
        Personnel and Training

From   Robert Mason, Divisional Manager
        Information Systems

Ref   RM/ST

Date   7 December 1994

PC TRAINING COURSES

As the PC courses proved so popular this year I propose to
run similar courses commencing in March 1995. I enclose a
copy of the draft programme for your information and comment.
As you will see, the courses will include 2 follow-up courses
for those who attended this year.

Also enclosed is a copy of my article about the future
development of PCs. I hope this will be published in the
next edition of the house magazine.

As voice-activated PCs require special dictating techniques,
I wonder if we should discuss courses in dictating techniques
for managers. We should introduce these courses gradually
over the next few years rather than wait until such PCs are
standard. They could result in better production from those
still using shorthand and audio.

Perhaps we could discuss these suggestions further.

Enc

Unit 5
PSC December 1994 Check Copies

Comlon International plc

Comlon House West Street London SW1Y 2AR

tel: 0181 302 0261
telex: Comlond 888941   telemessages: Comlond London SW1   fax: 0181 302 4169

DRAFT PROGRAMME

PC TRAINING COURSES 1995

COURSE 1

Using a PC - A course for beginners

Duration: 2 days

0900-1600 Saturday 4 March and 11 March

COURSE 2

Everyday DOS (for those who have completed the first course)

Duration: 1 day

0900-1630 Saturday 18 March

COURSE 3

Advanced DOS
(This course follows on from the basic course Everyday DOS.)

Duration: 1 day

0900-1630 Saturday 25 March

COURSE 4

Word for Windows
(This course offers an intensive introduction to the features
and facilities of Windows. A basic knowledge of computers and
familiarity with a computer keyboard is assumed.)

Duration: 2 days

0900-1600 Saturdays 1 April and 8 April

RM/ST
7 December 1994

Unit 5
PSC December 1994 Check Copies

M E M O R A N D U M

To   All Senior Managers

From Robert Mason, Divisional Manager
       Information Systems

Ref   RM/ST

Date 7 December 1994

NEW LAPTOP NOTEBOOKS

All next week I shall have in my department 4 demonstration
models of the latest laptop notebooks. Managers are welcome
to visit the department at any time between 1000 and 1200 or
from 1400 to 1600 Monday to Friday to view and operate these
models. Members of my staff will be available to demonstrate
the functions and answer questions.

I give below details of the 4 models on display. Please
telephone my secretary if you enquire further details.

Model	Mbyte hard disk	Mbyte memory	Features
Travel Companion 50	200	8	Mono; Windows, roller-ball mouse
Travel Companion 40	200	8	Colour screen; Windows
Compacta 20	40	2	Mono; can be upgraded to 4 RAM
Carrimate 25	80	4	Mono; lightweight carrying case

Unit 5
PSC December 1994 Check Copies

Comlon International plc

Comlon House West Street London SW1Y 2AR

tel: 0181 302 0261
telex: Comlond 888941   telemessages: Comlond London SW1   fax: 0181 302 4169

RM/ST

7 December 1994

Mr Paul Chan
Head of Buying Department
Comlon International plc
15 Harbour Road
Hong Kong

Dear Paul

WORD PROCESSING SYSTEMS

I refer to your fax 0824171. I am pleased to hear that you
expect to visit us soon. Please call me when you are in
London so that we can arrange to have lunch and discuss your
word processing needs further.

The first word processors were very simple. All the program
had to do was imitate the action of an electric typewriter and
add the boon of editing capacity.

In the beginning the dedicated word processor made all the
running but in the past few years word processing programs
have improved so that they are now better than dedicated word
processors.

The main line programs are so powerful that they are minor
desktop publishing programs. However it has been said that
only 20 per cent of the users use 80 per cent of the features
and 80 per cent of the users only bother with 20 per cent of
the features.

It is important to decide what you need and then to find the
equipment and programs which suit your requirements.

I look forward to meeting you. I shall be pleased to help in
any way I can.

Yours sincerely

ROBERT MASON
Divisional Manager
Information Systems

Unit 5
PSC December 1994 Check Copies

ARTICLE FOR HOUSE MAGAZINE

TAKE A LETTER - VOICE-ACTIVATED PC

My secretary sat in front of a laptop computer with a
microphone held to the corner of her mouth by a headband.
She spoke distinctly with each word clearly separated from
the next. She dictated the commas, fullstops and paragraphs.
As she spoke her words appeared on the screen in synchronisation with her voice.

She dictated until there were 200 words on the screen.
Though she is not an absolute beginner the system is new to
her and she only managed about 40 words a minute. More
experienced users have exceeded normal copy typing speed.

What has allowed voice recognition systems to get beyond the
area of interesting experimentation to commercial use has
been the phenomenal increase in speed, power and memory
capacity of the modern personal computer. This power and
speed is essential.

If you dictate a word into a computer two separate levels of
action are required. The first is for the computer to look
up the word in its list of acceptable words and that can mean
a very substantial vocabulary indeed. If the program finds
the word it will be displayed on the screen for the dictator
to approve.

Dictating in a slightly staccato way is not difficult but a
major problem arises because so many English words are
pronounced in the same way but spelled differently. The
computer has to make the selection by studying the context in
which the word appears. It has to do this at a speed which
is close to instantaneous so that the dictator does not have
to wait to see that the correct decision has been made.

It is important to understand that the system is not a
substitute for all typing. It is a substitute for dictation.
Typing is much quicker and much less prone to mistakes. The
dictator sees the results on the screen and can use macros to
call up all types of word and add, amend and improve. The
importance cannot be measured by merely comparing such a
system with a typist's speed; it has to be judged over the
whole process.

I can foresee the day when this system is standard on most new
office computers.

RM/ST
7 December 1994

Unit 5
PSC December 1994 Check Copies

Comlon International plc

Comlon House West Street London SW1Y 2AR

tel: 0181 302 0261
telex: Comlond 888941   telemessages: Comlond London SW1   fax: 0181 302 4169

RM/ST

7 December 1994

Ms Clare Watson
c/o Monsieur Jean Bouchon
Directeur
Boutique Express SA
117 rue de Seine
75008 Paris
France

Dear Ms Watson

PC TRAINING COURSES

Thank you for your letter of 5 December. I am pleased to
hear that you found your PC training course for beginners so
useful.

As the Saturday PC courses have proved so popular, similar
courses are proposed for 1995. A draft programme is enclosed,
from which you will note the special follow-up courses for
those who have completed the first courses.

As the advanced courses do not begin until 18 March, you could
arrange to stay in France until the end of February if you
wish.

Please telephone me when you return to Head Office. I will
arrange for you to attend the advanced course you choose.

Yours sincerely

ROBERT MASON
Divisional Manager
Information Systems

Enc

Unit 5
SSC December 1994 Check Copies

Comlon International plc

Comlon House West Street London SW1Y 2AR

tel: 0181 302 0261
telex: Comlond 888941   telemessages: Comlond London SW1   fax: 0181 302 4169

BF/ST

30 November 1994

Mr Alan Hunter
c/o Hotel Syon
118 rue de Vaugirard
07006 Paris
France

Dear

CONFERENCE FOR REGIONAL MANAGERS

I have concluded arrangements for this conference which is being held on 28 January 1995. An outline programme is enclosed, a copy of which has been sent to each manager.

A detailed programme will be enclosed in the conference wallet which will also contain copies of handouts supplied by the conference speakers, together with information about the social events which have been arranged.

I was pleased to hear that you will be back from France in time to attend the Reception and Dinner in the Waterloo Room of the Wellington Hotel on Friday 27 January. As you will see from the enclosed copy of my memo to all Regional Managers, Mr Nigel Baker, Managing Director of Freshglo Products Inc, has accepted my invitation to be the Guest Speaker.

Thank you very much for agreeing to propose the vote of thanks. My secretary will send you biographical details about Mr Baker nearer the date.

Yours sincerely

BEN FREEMAN
Store Operations Director

Enc

Unit 5
SSC December 1994 Check Copies

```
M E M O R A N D U M

To    All Regional Managers

From  Ben Freeman, Store Operations Director

Ref   BF/ST

Date  30 November 1994

ANNUAL CONFERENCE FOR REGIONAL MANAGERS

A one day conference will be held in the Comlon Conference
Centre on Saturday 28 January 1995.  All Regional Managers are
expected to attend.

The conference will cover a wide range of subjects including
future developments and marketing strategy.  An outline
programme is enclosed for your information.

Accommodation for the nights of Friday 27 January and
Saturday 28 January has been arranged at the Wellington
Hotel, West Street.  The hotel is within walking distance
of Comlon House.

The conference includes all meals from dinner on Friday until
Sunday breakfast.  Managers may check in to the hotel at any
time after noon on Friday 27 January.  Check-out time on
Sunday 29 January has been extended to 1800 to enable
managers to spend the day in London if they wish to do so.

A Reception and Dinner will be held in the Waterloo Room of
the Wellington Hotel on Friday 27 January, 1900 for 1930.
The Guest Speaker will be Mr Nigel Baker, Managing Director,
Freshglo Products Inc.

On Saturday 28 January a buffet supper will be served in the
hotel between 1830 and 2000.  Tickets have been obtained for
the evening performance of MISS SAIGON at the Theatre Royal,
Drury Lane on this date.  As the number of tickets is limited
only those attending the conference may apply.  Please
complete the tear-off slip and return to my secretary before
14 December.

Travelling expenses to and from the conference can be claimed
in the usual way.

Enc
```
- -
```
Please return by 14 December 1994 to
Secretary to Mr Ben Freeman, Store Operations Director,
Comlon International plc
Comlon House, West Street, London SW1Y 2AR

Please reserve a ticket for me to attend MISS SAIGON on
Saturday 28 January 1995.

NAME ........................... AREA ......................

Signature ..................... Date ......................
```

Unit 5
SSC December 1994 Check Copies

```
CONFERENCE FOR REGIONAL MANAGERS

SATURDAY 28 JANUARY 1995

CONFERENCE CENTRE, COMLON HOUSE



0900        REGISTRATION

0930        WELCOME AND INTRODUCTION TO THE CONFERENCE
            Ben Freeman, Store Operations Director

0945        STORE SECURITY - FROM SHOPLIFTING TO TERRORISM
            Robert Hughes, Security Controller

1015        COFFEE

1045        FRESHGLO PRODUCTS - VIDEO AND SALES PRESENTATION
            Peter Hill, Sales Manager, Freshglo Products Inc

1130        LAUNCHING THE NEW FRESHGLO RANGE
            David Hayes, Marketing Controller

1230        LUNCH - SENIOR MANAGEMENT DINING ROOM

1400        NEW DEVELOPMENTS IN STAFF TRAINING
            Sarah King, Personnel Controller

1445        HEALTHY STAFF IN A SAFE ENVIRONMENT
            Maria Lopez, Health and Safety Controller

1530        BRAINS TRUST - DISCUSSION OF CURRENT PROBLEMS
            Panel:  Robert Hughes, Sarah King,
                    Maria Lopez, Ben Freeman

1600        TEA




BF/ST
30 November 1994
```

Unit 5
SSC December 1994 Check Copies

```
CONFERENCE FOR REGIONAL MANAGERS

NOTES FOR WELCOME AND INTRODUCTION



WELCOME REGIONAL MANAGERS



INTRODUCE NEW MANAGERS

     Bill Norman
     Len Richards



CONGRATULATIONS AND AWARD TO

     Rose Smith for best sales results 1994
     John Ellis for best window display



INTRODUCE STAFF SPEAKERS - EMPHASISE CONFERENCE AIMS

     Robert Hughes, Security Controller
     David Hayes, Marketing Controller
     Sarah King, Personnel Controller
     Maria Lopez, Health and Safety Controller



BRIEF SUMMARY OF ACHIEVEMENTS AND PROBLEMS DURING PAST YEAR

     New stores in north west and south east
     National training awards
     Mention firebombs in Birmingham and Manchester



FUTURE DEVELOPMENTS

     Negotiations for new sites in Midlands
     Continual need for security vigilance
     Freshglo franchise, regional launches, handout
     for use in each area



BF/ST
30 November 1994
```

Unit 5
SSC December 1994 Check Copies

Comlon International plc

Comlon House West Street London SW1Y 2AR

tel: 0181 302 0261
telex: Comlond 888941   telemessages: Comlond London SW1   fax: 0181 302 4169

BF/ST

30 November 1994

The Manager
Wellington Hotel
West Street
London
SW1Y 2BX

Dear Sir

CONFIRMATION OF RESERVATION

I confirm the reservations made by telephone as follows:

DATE(S)	Friday 27 January to Sunday 29 January 1995
FUNCTION	Conference for Regional Managers
NUMBER OF BEDROOMS	11

NAMES OF GUESTS

Ben Freeman	Maria Lopez
Kate Green	Bill Norman
Robert Hughes	Len Richards
John Ellis	Rose Smith
David Hayes	Mary Wyatt
Sarah King	

MEALS

27 January - Reception and Dinner
28 January - Breakfast
            Buffet Supper
29 January - Breakfast

SPECIAL REQUIREMENTS   Extended checkout agreed to 1800
                            on 29 January

ACCOUNTS TO   Accounts Department

ENQUIRIES TO   Mr Freeman's secretary, extension 205

Detailed requirements for the Reception and Dinner on Friday
27 January and the Buffet Supper on Saturday 28 January are
given in my letter reference BF/ST dated 1 September.

Yours faithfully

BEN FREEMAN
Store Operations Director

Unit 5
SSC December 1994 Check Copies

Comlon International plc

Comlon House West Street London SW1Y 2AR

tel: 0181 302 0261
telex: Comlond 888941   telemessages: Comlond London SW1   fax: 0181 302 4169

CONFERENCE HANDOUT

FRESHGLO TOILETRIES

Comlon International plc is pleased to announce that agreement has been reached with Freshglo Products Inc for an exclusive franchise to sell the new range of Freshglo toiletries in the 600 Comlon stores throughout the UK.

FRESHGLO products conform to strict Comlon standards and are formulated without animal testing.

The range of products includes

Hair shampoos, conditioners and styling mousses with specific cosmetic agents to protect hair, maintain style, and preserve softness and shine.

Face and hand creams and moisturisers with added sunscreen to protect delicate skin and enhance texture. Available in full fragrance range or fragrance-free.

Perfume, toilet water, after shave, body lotion, and talc deodorants in the following fragrances. Unscented deodorants are also available.

FOR HIM Serge, Corduroy, Tartan, Black Leather

FOR HER Chiffon, Silk, Velvet, Linen

Cosmetic packs containing mascara, lipstick, blusher and nail enamel in 2 varieties

AUTUMN for those who wear mainly reds, browns and oranges

SPRING for those who prefer to wear pastel shades

The full range of FRESHGLO toiletries will be on sale at your local Comlon Store from 1 March 1995.

Free demonstrations and advice will be given.

BF/ST
30 November 1994

Printers' correction signs

Mark in the Margin	Meaning	Mark in the Text
℘	Delete (leave out) the character or word(s) indicated	/ or —
⋏	Insert the character or word(s) where indicated	⋏
#	Insert a space where indicated	⋏
close up	Close up the space where indicated	⌣
uc caps OR	Use upper case (capitals) for the letter(s) indicated	—
lc	Use lower case (small letters) for the letter(s) indicated	—
trs	Transpose (change round) the order of the words as indicated	∽
NP	Begin a new paragraph	[OR //
stet	(Let it stand) Transcribe the word(s) originally crossed out	- - - - - -
/-/	Insert a hyphen	⋏
/–/	Insert a dash	⋏
⌒,	Insert a comma	⋏
⊙	Insert a full stop	⋏
᾿⁄	Insert single quotation marks	⋏
ˮ⁄	Insert double quotation marks	⋏

Index